SEEING

WITH

JESUS' EYES

Testomonials from Fr. Lange's students, friends, and admirers

I have known Fr. Lange for many years and have always appreciated his sense of humor and pastoral insights. We frequently meet for breakfast at a local café where Father Lange shares his wisdom on topics ranging from Catholic doctrine and ecumenism to baseball and local history. And frequently I'm made privy to a sermon that he is diligently composing for an upcoming weekend Mass at a local parish. I truly appreciate Father's paternal guidance as experienced in his countless articles in the Catholic Herald or in a shared cup of delicious decafe coffee. Thank you for your friendship and for your love of the priesthood.

– John Leonard Berg
Cuba City, WI

Growing up and going to school at St. Joseph School in Sinsinawa, Wi. Fr. Don Lange taught me about the stigmata of some bold Saints and moved me to contemplate that when he held up the Eucharist. He also taught me to be on the lookout for a hard inside fastball when he was pitching. Praise God for Fr. Lange and his gifts!"

– Ryan Berning

Faithful, Committed, Humble, Compassionate, Focused, Understanding, Grounded, Unassuming, Forgiving, Humorous are words that in total describe the Christ filled heart and soul of my good friend Father Don Lange.

– Deacon Bill Bussan

As I worked with Fr. Lange before and after Masses, I learned of his gentleness and steadiness if something didn't go as we wanted or planned it to in the preparation or after the Mass. His gentleness touched all of us. Fr. Lange immersed himself in his study of the books of the Bible so completely that he was able to convey to us the 'whole picture' as he told this story in his sermon to all. Fr. Lange also had a sense of humor as he sometimes called me 'Joan of Arc' as we were working together.

– Joan McCauley

We wanted to say that we really enjoy Fr. Donald Lange's column that's in the *Catholic Herald*. We really congratulate him on his years of service to God and the Catholic church

– Mr. and Mrs. Francis Deutsch

Delivered by Gabriel
Dear Pam,
Fr. Lange has permission to eat in the halls because of his tremendous need for energy in his teaching. Also, on Wednesdays he eats a late breakfast.
    With love,
    Abba

P.S. Be good in his class and you will heap up treasures in heaven.

I received the above note in my locker at Beloit Catholic High the day after reminding Fr. Lange of the school policy, "no eating in the hall!" I was honored that Gabriel, the Messenger Angel, would take the time to deliver me a note from Abba. Like the Angel Gabriel, Fr. Lange always made time to share God's love with students, teachers, and all those he encountered, either in class, in the hall, or in Mass. To me, Fr. Lange has always been a model of humble service, eating in the hall—caring more for the needs of others than his own.

    When I was sixteen, I asked Fr. Lange to help me coordinate a retreat for my classmates, because none were being offered. Because of his "yes" my peers and I were given the opportunity to plan and realize a retreat unique to our needs. The groundwork was laid, the importance of retreat was instilled, and as a parish minister I have had the honor of facilitating many retreats for youth and adults, hopefully offering others the same experience of encountering God that Fr. Lange offered me and my peers thirty eight years ago. Thank you Fr. Lange.

– Pam Peiffer Sirinek

When I was his student I noticed that Fr. Lange had a particular gift: the optimism to guide teenagers on their faith journeys without becoming disheartened. As I grew older I realized that optimism was grounded in a deep trust in God, and that it extended beyond high school students to everyone who Fr. Lange encounters. By presenting some of the insights and meditations that Fr. Lange has shared throughout his life as a priest, this book provides a glimpse into his gentle spirit and strong faith.

– Polly Onderak Schmidt
Beloit Catholic High

Father Lange has a very special way of taking the word of God, adding his wit and a life lesson to make it so meaningful. Thank you Father for bringing each of us a little closer to God with your down to earth articles.

– Mary Jo Loeffelholz

I have known Fr. Lange for most of my 60 years and have always known him to be a humble servant with a keen eye for observing the way God is present in all our lives. This collection of essays is a great example of his power of observation and his servants heart. Thank you for sharing these with us Father!

– Tim McKearn
Beloit

Fr. Lange has a gift that many, including myself, may be envious of—the gift of writing. I look forward to, not only the holidays, but also special celebration days throughout the year, knowing Fr. Lange will have a memorable written selection in the local newspaper. Each story always provides me with a lasting inspiration for whom it was written. Thank you, Fr. Lange, for your special gift!

– Mary Mowry

SEEING

WITH

JESUS' EYES

By

Fr. Donald Lange

Seeing with Jesus' Eyes © 2020 Fr. Donald Lange. All rights reserved. No part of this publication may be reproduced, distributed, or transmitted in any form or by any means, including photocopying, recording, or other electronic or mechanical methods, without the prior written permission of the publisher, except in the case of brief quotations embodied in critical reviews and certain other noncommercial uses permitted by copyright law. For permission requests, write to the publisher, addressed "Attention: Permissions Coordinator," at the address below.

Much of the material which follows was originally published in the *Madision Catholic Herald*.

Forty Press, LLC
427 Van Buren Street
Anoka, MN 55303
www.fortypress.com

ISBN 978-1-938473-33-3

Dedication

I thank the Venerable Father Samuel Mazzuchelli who embodied the Christian values I tried to share in the book's articles. He saw with the eyes of Jesus and loved with the heart of Jesus. I get tired just thinking about what God accomplished through him. Though he died on February 23, 1864, his example influences believers today, including me. I had the privilege of serving at St. Patrick Parish in Benton, Wisconsin, where he served and died. Before I celebrate mass there, I always visit his grave. For these and other reasons, I dedicate the book to him and join thousands in praying for his beatification.

TABLE OF CONTENTS

- 10   Foreword
- 11   Introduction
- 13   PART I: ADVENT
- 23   PART II: CHRISTMAS / NEW YEARS SEASON
- 39   PART III: ORDINARY TIME
  - Pro-Life
  - Vocations
  - Dr. Martin Luther King
  - Unity
  - Catholic Schools Week
- 63   PART IV: LENT
- 75   PART V: SPRING
  - St. Joseph
  - Easter
  - Mother's Day
  - Earth Day
  - Memorial Day
- 113   PART VI: SUMMER
  - Feasts
  - Father's Day
  - Independence Day
  - Assumption
  - Sports
  - Labor Day
- 158   PART VII: FALL
  - Grandparents
  - Fall Saints
  - Holy Rosary
  - Fall of Our Lives
  - All Saints & All Souls Day
  - Thanksgiving
  - Feast of Christ the King
- 194   PART VIII: FR. SAMUEL MAZZUCHELLI
- 200   ADDENDUM
- 207   ACKNOWLEDGMENTS
- 208   ABOUT THE AUTHOR

Foreword

The first time I met Fr. Don Lange I was a new altar boy in the 5th grade and he was a new priest filling it at my parish in Beloit, Wisconsin. I remember telling my mom afterwards that I wasn't sure who was more nervous, me or Fr. Lange. My first impression that day of Fr. Lange was that he was a kind and sincere man, qualities that remain true to this day.

There was no way to know that day that I served Mass for Fr. Lange what an important role he would play in my life. Fr. Lange would eventually be one of my high school religion teachers and my freshman baseball coach. Years later when I returned to Beloit Catholic High School as a teacher Fr. Lange would serve as a colleague, mentor and friend. We have remained friends ever since.

This book is a collection of essays written by Fr. Lange over the years. Most of these were originally published in the *Catholic Herald* as part of his regular column that appeared in that publication. The book is laid out to follow the church calendar so whatever season of the year we are in you can return to this book and find reflections on Advent, Easter, Mother's Day, Father's Day, and many other church and secular topics of interest.

The columns appear in the book as they did in the *Catholic Herald* which means that occasionally you'll find that Father has favorite quotes and anecdotes he returns to that help him illustrate his thoughts. We debated as to whether or not to remove some of these repeated thoughts and decided to leave them exactly as they originally appeared.

There is something about Fr. Lange's writing that makes his message, relatable and accessible. And like the first day I met him, his kindness shines through in everything he writes. One get's the sense that as he was writing these essays that he understood what his readers might be going through in their own lives and that he was speaking to each reader on their own level in a very personal way.

I have enjoyed revisiting each of these columns. Reading them again has felt like getting reconnected to old friends. I hope you'll enjoy them as well.

– Tim McKearn

Introduction

Good things often happen during a meal. At the Last supper, during a Passover meal, Jesus gave us the Eucharist and said, "Do this in memory of me." Good things happened to me over another meal. Tim McKearn, one of my former students, drove sixty miles to treat me to dinner. During the meal, I mentioned how I had wanted to put together some of my writings from the Catholic Herald in a book but apparently it was not going to happen. Tim listened. Six years later, he called and asked whether I would be interested in publishing a book of my Catholic Herald articles. He stated that since the articles held his interest and helped him to live his faith, it might do the same for others. Best of all, he also offered to help put the book together. This was good news!

We quickly formed a committee consisting of Tim, Mary Jo Loeffelholz and me. We soon discovered that this task was more challenging than it first seemed; but thanks to the Holy Spirit, we persevered, and the book was completed. The Holy Spirit helped us to do what we cannot do by ourselves. It is my hope that the book helps readers and myself to see with Jesus' eyes and live a more meaningful life in this world because of our belief in Heaven.

Like the Catholic Herald, the book follows the church year, beginning with Advent and Christmas and continuing to Ordinary time, Lent, Easter, and ending with the Feast of Chris the King. Under each season are some articles not directly connected with the season, but they do reflect Christian values. The articles express the Christian belief that Jesus answers basic questions of life: "Who am I? Where am I going and why?"

Who am I? God reveals that we and fellow humans are created in the divine image. Since God is love, we image God best when we love; consequently, we should treat each other with respect for we are our brother's and sister's keeper. Pablo Casals, the great musician for peace, asked a baby, "Do you know who you are? You are a marvel – you are unique. There has never been another exactly like you in the millions of years that have passed. You are a masterpiece! Your legs, your arms, your cunning little fingers. You may become a Michelangelo, a Shakespeare, a Beethoven. You have the capacity for anything.

When you grow up, will you harm another like you?"

Since we image God who is love, we Christians are to love God with our heart, mind, and soul and our neighbor as self. In John 4:20, it says, "If you do not love your brother whom you can see, how can you love God whom you cannot see?"

Where am I going? It is hoped that these articles will help the reader and myself to see that we are pilgrims on a journey through time to Heaven. Earth is our temporary home and Heaven our eternal home.

Why? The articles show that God has a plan for each of us designed to help us live the gospel in today's world that often embraces philosophies that tell us that we do not need God. Scripture tells us that God made us to know Him, love Him, and be happy with Him in this world and the next – Heaven. That is his plan for us.

One characteristic of the book's articles is stories and examples connecting Christian values with human experience. We humans seem wired for stories. Jesus used stories to connect his teaching with human experience. One of the greatest stories ever told is the parable of the prodigal son which connects and contrasts the forgiveness of the earthly father and the unforgiveness of the elder brother with the forgiveness of our Heavenly Father. I am glad that God is a forgiving Father. This gives me hope.

I: ADVENT

1. Contemplating Mary's Spiritual Beauty

During October 1863, Fr. Samuel Mazzuchelli received a vision from Mary as he rode to Shullsburg with three Dominican Sisters for the sacrament of Confirmation. He told Fr. John Kinsella, his confessor, "I have always been an admirer of beauty. But never have I seen anything that compared with the beauty of God's mother."

Feast of Immaculate Conception

We recognize Mary's beauty and grace on December 8 when we celebrate the feast of the Immaculate Conception. Mary's Immaculate Conception was proclaimed as dogma by Pope Pius IX on December 8, 1854.

In No. 491 of the *Catechism of the Catholic Church*, Pius IX is quoted: "The most Blessed Virgin Mary was, from the first moment of her conception, by a singular grace and privilege of Almighty God and by virtue of the merits of Jesus Christ, Savior of the human race, preserved immune from all stain of original sin."

God gifted Mary with freedom from sin so that she might be the mother of Jesus. God sent the angel Gabriel to ask Mary if she would freely consent to be mother of the messiah, the dream of most Jewish girls. Mary responded, "I am the servant of the Lord. Let it be done to me as you say."

Beauty in Virtue

Some say that expectant mothers are beautiful. Mary's face surely radiated the joy of carrying Jesus in her heart and womb. Her beauty touched stony hearts. Even unborn John leaped with joy in his mother's womb.

The beauty of Mary's Immaculate Conception should not blind us to sin's evil. Sin often tempts us under the guise of an apparent good. But it taints the beauty of God's image, wounds our ability to love, and causes violence to multiply. Mortal sin can rob us of the priceless gift of eternal life.

Mary's consent enabled her to be the mother of Jesus who would redeem us from sin, offer us the gift of eternal life, and send the Holy Spirit to help us live a Christ-like life.

Pope John Paul II and Pope Benedict XVI stated that Mary is the mother of priests because she is the mother of Jesus, the high priest. Priests are stewards of Christ's love as the Good Shepherd.

Mary gave us Jesus, and she is also his greatest disciple. There is beauty in virtue, and Mary, full of grace, lived a life of Christ-like virtue. William Wordsworth described her as "our tainted nature's solitary boast."

Mary is who we would be if not for original sin. A student told me that if she could be anyone else, she would like to be Mary. She is the perfect reflection of Jesus. Mary is the beautiful reed through whom the Spirit breathed Jesus' love.

As Jesus' disciple, Mary followed him to the cross. As she stood under the cross, Jesus commissioned Mary to be our spiritual mother who intercedes and cares for us. We Catholics honor Mary as our Blessed Mother.

"Do What He Tells You"

Parents who lose children can identify with Mary and Joseph, who lost Jesus in the temple and later to a cruel death on the cross. She understands our suffering because she has been there.

Like Jesus, Mary went about doing good. She hurried to help Elizabeth prepare for the birth of John, the Baptist. She gave birth to Jesus in a smelly stable that would be condemned by today's health departments.

At Cana, she interceded with Jesus on behalf of the couple to avoid them embarrassment. Her words to the waiter, "Do what he tells you," is one of the best and shortest homilies ever given.

Like Mary, we Catholics are graced. Unlike Mary, we sin, but God redeemed us. Like Mary we strive to do Gods' will and help modern Elizabeths or others in need. We join our suffering with the suffering of Jesus, as did Mary.

Waiting Patiently During Advent

Mary is the patroness of Advent who waited and longed to give birth to Jesus and offer him to the world. During Advent we join Mary in waiting patiently for the coming of Jesus at Christmas.

Fr. Kevin O'Shea stated that Mary was so in love with God that she conceived Christ in her heart before her womb. Like Mary, we are called to spiritually conceive Christ through the Holy Spirit and share him with others. Advent challenged us to renew our efforts to be Jesus' disciples and stewards.

Mary is patroness of the United States under the title of the Immaculate Conception. The lyrics of "America the Beautiful" praise America's cornucopia of blessings. Yet its words "May God mend thine every flaw" invite us to continuous conversion.

May the grave beauty of Mary's life that motivated the Venerable Father Mazzuchelli help us to be committed Catholics and responsible citizens like him. May we celebrate Advent and Christmas with Mary's faith and joy.

Have a Mary Day.

2: Mary Inspires Us to Live a Fruitful Advent

The word Advent comes from the Latin word *adventus*, which means "coming." During Advent we wait patiently for the coming of Jesus.

According the *General Norms for the Liturgical Year and Calendar*, Advent has a two-fold character. It is a season to prepare for Christmas when we remember Christ's first coming to us.

It is also a season when that first remembrance directs our minds and hearts to remember Christ's second coming at the end of time. Advent is thus a season of devout and joyful expectation.

Model of Advent Waiting

Mary is the model of Advent waiting for us, because she joyfully, prayerfully, and patiently waited for the birth of Jesus whom she carried in her womb close to her heart.

One of my grade school classmates was born on Christmas. His mother could identify with Mary. Both longed to give birth and share their son with the world.

Fr. Kevin O'Shea, a Marian expert, said that Mary was so in love with Jesus that she conceived him in her heart before she conceived him in her womb.

It was the dream of devout Jewish girls to be the mother of the messiah. God the Father chose Mary by asking her to be Jesus' mother. Mary's consent enabled her to be the mother of Jesus, who would redeem us from sin, offer us the gift of eternal life, and send the Holy Spirit to help us to live a Christ-like life.

Radiating Joy

Some say that expectant mothers' faces are beautiful. Mary's face surely radiated the joy of carrying Jesus in her heart and womb. Her beauty touched stony hearts. Even unborn John leaped with joy in his mother's womb.

Mary's Immaculate Conception has become one of the most popular Marian devotions. Many dioceses and churches have Mary as their patron saint under the title of the Immaculate Conception as does my home parish in Kieler, Wis.

In 1846, the First Council of Baltimore declared Mary to be patroness of the United States under the title of the Immaculate Conception. The patronal church of the United States is the Basilica of the National Shrine of the Immaculate Conception, dedicated to Mary, and located in Washington, D.C. It is the largest Roman Catholic church in North America, and one of the 10 largest in the world.

Preparing for Christmas

Mary's patient waiting can inspire us to patiently use Advent to prepare for Jesus' birth at Christmas. Above all, Advent can help us come closer to Jesus. Confession, devotions, prayer, spiritual reading, visiting shut-ins, participating more fully in Mass, and other good works help us to prepare for the coming of Jesus. The Holy Spirit will show us other ways if we ask.

Advent listening in faith helps us to let God guide us in our journey through the sometimes-dark days of December to the light of Christmas hope.

It helps us to prepare a crib in the inn of our heart, so that we can joyfully receive Jesus, the Word made flesh, at Christmas and then keep him by giving Him away.

May we enjoy a blessed Advent of hope that helps us to celebrate one of our best Christmases ever!

3: Immaculate Conception Points to Advent

Franz Werfel wrote a popular book called *The Song of Bernadette*. The reason he wrote this book goes back to World War II

Shrine at Lourdes, France

As a controversial Jew in occupied France, he was on the Nazi hit list. He and Alma, his wife, fled from the Nazis who pursued them. They sought shelter in Lourdes where the famous shrine of Mary is located. One night he went alone to the shrine.

In the darkness, he prayed, "God, I'm not a believer. I must be honest and say so. I am a Jew. But in my extreme need, on the chance that I could be wrong, I ask you to help me and my wife. If you see us safely to the United States, I promise to write a story of Lourdes for all the world to read." After that prayer, he experiences peace of mind that he never before experienced. His prayer was answered.

He and his wife found their way into Spain. A few days later, they were safely on a ship sailing to the United States. He kept his promise and wrote the book *The Song of Bernadette*.

When Mary appeared to Bernadette at Lourdes, Bernadette did not know the identity of this beautiful lady. Mary revealed herself to Bernadette when she told her, "I am the Immaculate Conception." Mary's appearances to Bernadette reinforced the dogma of the Immaculate Conception, which Pope Pius IX had proclaimed three and half years earlier. We celebrate the feast of the Immaculate Conception on December 8.

Definition of the Doctrine

On December 8, 1854, Pope Pius IX solemnly declared that Mary was conceived free from original sin and that this was now a dogma of faith to be believed by all the faithful. In No. 491 of the *Catechism of the Catholic Church*, Pius IX proclaimed: "The most Blessed Virgin Mary was, from the first moment of her conception, by a singular grace and privilege of Almighty God and by virtue of the merits of Jesus Christ, Savior of the human race, preserved immune from all stain of original sin."

From all women, God chose Mary who was sinless to be the mother of the sinless one. God sent the angel Gabriel to ask Mary if she would freely consent to be Jesus' mother. In Luke 1:34-35 Mary asked the angel, "How can this be since I have no relations with a man?" The angel explained, "The Holy Spirit will come upon you and the Power of the Most High will overshadow you. Therefore, the child to be born will be called holy, the Son of God."

After the angel's explanation, Mary answered, "Behold, I am the handmaid of the Lord. May it be done to me according to your word." It was the dream of Jewish girls to be the Messiah's mother. God freely chose sinless Mary to be Jesus' mother because she was fully open to God's will and full of God's grace and of the Immaculate Conception.

Patroness of the USA

We pray to Mary, immaculately conceived, the patroness of the United States, to watch over our country and protect it. The lyrics of "America the Beautiful" praise America's cornucopia of blessings. But its words "May God mend thine every flaw" invite us to continuous conversion to being more Christ-like.

Mary is the patroness of Advent. She waited and longed to give birth to Jesus and offer him to the world. In 1864, at the Sixth Provincial Council of Baltimore, the bishops of the United States adopted a decree by which they chose the Virgin Mary conceived without sin as patroness of the United States under the title of the Immaculate Conception. Fr. Kevin O'Shea stated that Mary was so in love with God that she conceived Christ in her heart before her womb.

Preparation During Advent

Advent invites us to grow in our unique vocation as Jesus' disciples. We spiritually conceive and receive Christ through Baptism and share him with others in ways no one else can where we live, work, or recreate.

During Advent we join Mary in waiting patiently for the birth of Jesus at Christmas. We can prepare for Christmas and for Christ's second coming by participating in Mass and Advent devotions, receiving the sacrament of Reconciliation, giving food to the poor, spiritual reading, and perhaps reading or re-reading *The Song of Bernadette*.

The Holy Spirit will show us other ways if we ask for his guidance. On this patronal feast of our country we can also join other

Americans in appreciating God as the source of our many blessings as the Blessed Mother did.

4: Ten Ways to Help Us Live a Fruitful Advent

The word "Advent" comes from the Latin word *adventus* which means "coming", "arrival" or "visit". The Advent season begins four Sundays before Christmas and lasts between three and four weeks, depending upon which weekday Christmas happens to be celebrated in a certain year. Advent is a time of prayerful, patient waiting and preparation for Jesus' birth. We can prepare to celebrate Jesus' birth by reading the New Testament infancy narratives, reflecting upon the Old Testament prophecies of Jesus' coming and in other ways.

During Advent as we prepare to celebrate Christ's first coming at Christmas, we also look forward to Jesus' second coming. In addition, we try to recognize and respond to Christ's daily comings in our life.

Advent is a season to renew and deepen our relationship with God. It offers us opportunities to step back from the consumerism and busyness of the materialistic world so we can receive the Advent grace that God wants to give us.

The following list offers some graced ways that we can use Advent to prepare for Christ's coming:

1. During Advent we can try to recognize and respond to local and global injustices.
2. We can contribute to a food pantry, support a third world child or write elected representatives on behalf of the poor.
3. We can visit someone who is lonely, ill, or neglected.
4. We can forgive wrongs done to us and ask forgiveness of those we have wronged.
5. We can be a peacemaker in our family and community and encourage those who are discouraged.
6. We can write a letter we have postponed. We can pray for those for whom no one else seems to pray.

7. We can deepen our personal relationship with God through prayer, spiritual reading and participation in Sunday and holy day Masses. If our schedule permits, we can participate in daily Mass and Eucharistic adoration.
8. We can light a candle each week on the Advent wreath to remind us that we are getting close to Christmas.
9. We can continue to be a faithful, loyal Catholic and live the Church's teachings.

May Advent prepare us to celebrate the birth of Jesus with the joy of Mary, the surprise and wonder of the shepherds and the song of the angels. May we continue to receive Christ in the crib of our heart and share him with others at Christmas and every day.

5: Advent Reconciliation

In the November 2013 issue of The Word Among Us, Scott Hahn is quoted as saying that an American priest went to Rome for a conference and a group meeting with Pope John Paul II. Before the meeting, the priest noticed a beggar on the steps of a church.

He recognized him as his former seminary classmate in Rome. They were ordained to the priesthood together. Now he was a beggar.

Response of St. John Paul II

When he met with the pope, the priest told him about his classmate. Pope John Paul promised to pray for him. Then he invited the priest and his beggar-classmate to dine with him.

When the meal ended, the pope asked if he could speak alone with the beggar. When they met privately, the beggar said that the pope clasped his hands and asked, "Father, would you hear my confession?"

"I'm a beggar," the man apologized.

The pope replied, "So am I! We're all beggars!"

After the beggar-priest heard the pope's confession, he knelt and tearfully asked the pope to hear his confession. The pope accepted. Receiving the Sacrament of Reconciliation from the pope filled him with joy.

Priests See the Joy of Reconciliation Often

We priests have seen the joy of the "forgiven beggar" in penitents who have been away from the Church for years and received the Sacrament of Reconciliation. Sometimes they seem to bubble with joy.

Advent is the season of hope and joy. During Advent we wait with hope and joy for Christ's second coming when He will come in glory to judge the living and the dead.

In No. 1060 of the Catechism of the Catholic Church it says, "At the end of time, the Kingdom of God will come in its fullness. Then the just will reign with Christ forever, glorified in body and soul, and the material universe itself will be transformed. God will then be 'all in all' (1 Corinthians 15:28), in eternal life."

From December 17 to December 24, the Mass readings shift from waiting for Christ's second coming to preparing to celebrate Christ's coming at Christmas.

Scriptural Reminders

In Luke 1:31, the angel Gabriel tells Mary, "You shall conceive and bear a son and give him the name Jesus." The name Jesus in Hebrew means "God saves." It reminds us that the Father gave us Jesus so that he would redeem us from our sins so that we might be reconciled with one another and the Father. After Jesus died on the cross, he returned to the Father and sent the Holy Spirit to help us love others as he loved us.

After the angel's visit, Mary visited Elizabeth who would soon give birth to John the Baptist. When Elizabeth heard Mary's greeting, unborn John in Elizabeth's womb recognized Jesus and leaped for joy. The adult John the Baptist prepared the way for Jesus' coming by preaching repentance.

Three Parables of Jesus

Chapter 15 of Luke consists of three parables of joyful repentance. In the Parable of the Lost Sheep, Jesus says "There is more joy in Heaven over one repentant sinner than 99 righteous people who have no need to repent."

Then Jesus ends the parable of the Lost Coin with the words, "There will be rejoicing among the angels of God over one repentant sinner."

The final parable in Luke 15 is the prodigal son. The father is so joyous over his son's repentant return that he sponsors a big feast to celebrate his coming home. When the elder brother hears the sound of music and dancing, he becomes angry. The loving Father explains to his elder son, "But (don't you see?) we had to celebrate and rejoice! This brother of yours was dead and had come to life. He was lost and has been found."

Penance is Powerful During Advent Season

It seems to me that communal penance services especially offer us the graced opportunity to celebrate the joy that comes from experiencing God's forgiveness, especially as revealed in Luke 15.

At Christmas we can show children the crib and explain that Jesus means "God saves." We can tell them that Jesus was born to redeem us from our sins and gift us with Heaven. We can remind ourselves that saying Jesus' name reverently helps us recognize again that the merits of his redemption are mediated to us in priest's absolution in the Sacrament of Penance.

The absolution begins with the words, "God, the Father of mercies, through the death and resurrection of his Son has reconciled the world to himself and sent the Holy Spirit among us for the forgiveness of sins." Alleluia! Rejoice!

Blessed Pope John Paul, who will be canonized on April 27, 2014, often went to confession. His example can motivate us to receive the Sacrament of Penance, which parishes offer at special times during Advent.

Confession Helps Us Celebrate Christmas with Joy

Receiving the Sacrament of Reconciliation during Advent helps us to celebrate Christmas with purified and joyful hearts. The best Christmas present that we can give to Jesus is the gift of a purified forgiving and forgiven heart. Let us pray for the grace to offer Jesus this gift this Christmas.

II: CHRISTMAS / NEW YEARS SEASON

1: The Greatest Gift of Christmas

Every time a baby is born, there is new hope for the human race. I learned this as a high school sophomore when my baby brother was born. What a miracle of grace! As I studied his perfectly formed hands and feet, I was filled with awe and hope. I wondered who he would grow up to be. I hoped that he would be bigger, stronger, more athletic, and more intelligent than I was. My sister hoped that he would grow up to be a gentleman.

New Hope for Humanity

When Jesus was born, there was new hope for humanity. God, the Father, looked at the human race whom he created in the divine image. The image of God in some of us had been so tarnished by sin that had God not been omniscient (all knowing), he would not have recognized his image.

We image God best when we love, but instead of loving each other as God intended, some humans commit sins of hate, jealousy, violence, and even murder. We humans needed to be redeemed from our sins.

Instead of condemning us, God, the Father, had compassion on us. In John 3:16, it says, "Yes, God so loved the world that God gave his only Son, that whoever believes in him will not die but may have eternal life. God did not send his Son into the world to condemn the world, but that the world might be saved through him."

God the Father sent Jesus to teach, to model, and to empower us to love. He died on the cross to redeem us from sin which keeps us from loving and ultimately hurts those whom we love. He sent the Holy Spirit to empower us to love as he loved.

Becoming a Helpless Baby

At birth, babies are among the most helpless of God's creatures. Without their parents' love, care, and protection, they would perish. The infant Jesus needed his parents to protect him.

When Herod tried to kill Jesus, Mary and Joseph fled to Egypt with him and became refugees. Today babies still need the care and protection of adults.

Babies Need Care, Protection

Millions of unborn babies are aborted each year. In baseball jargon, they are called out even before they have a chance to step up to the plate.

According to the World Health Organization, more than 10 million children under five also die each year. Most are from poor countries and most of their deaths could be prevented. Children's letters to Santa often reveal the hard times that American families are experiencing.

In recent years, children's letters to Santa often reveal the hard times that American families are experiencing. Instead of writing letters to Santa asking for toys and electronic gadgets, more children are asking that he bring their families basic essentials for Christmas such as food, school supplies and toiletries. These bare necessities shouldn't be Christmas luxuries. A Los Angeles child wrote to Santa. "Please bring Mommy some food. She's been good this year."

Our Gift to Jesus

At Christmas, we celebrate the Father's gift of Jesus who wants to offer us heaven. What can we give in appreciation of this priceless gift? The greatest gift that we can give to Jesus is to invite him into the crib of our heart.

Christina Rossetti expressed this in her simple but profound little poem, "What can I give him poor as I am, if I were a shepherd, I would give him a lamb. If I were a wiseman, I would do my part/ What can I give him? (I will) give him my heart!"

We give Jesus our heart when we accept him as Lord and Savior and follow his ways through time into eternity. To keep Jesus, we must give him away in Christ-like prayer, almsgiving, and loving service to others. When we do this, we make every day a little Christmas! Amen!

2: Silent Night Prepares to Celebrate Christmas

There are slightly different versions of the origin of the Christmas carol "Silent Night." My favorite version reveals that shortly before Christmas in 1818, Fr. Joseph Mohr discovered that the organ of St. Nicholas Church in Oberndorf, Austria, was broken. He knew that his parishioners would be disappointed without Christmas music.

Image of Mother and Baby

Earlier Father Mohr had traveled up the mountain to bring Communion to a woman who had just given birth. As he walked home past the beautiful snow covered slope, the image of the mother and her baby surfaced. They reminded him of Mary and the Christ child.

Inspired, he began to compose the lyrics of "Silent Night." Then he took the lyrics to the organist, Franz Gruber, who wrote the music for "Silent Night." It was first sung on Christmas to the accompaniment of a guitar.

The Greatest Gift

The Christmas season is a time of gift-giving. For Christmas, the greatest Christmas present is God the Father's gift of Jesus. In John 3:16 it says, "For God so loved the world that he gave us his holy Son so that everyone who believes in him might not perish but might enjoy eternal life."

Jesus became like us so we could become like him. He showed us how to live a Christ-like life. He died on the cross to redeem us from our sins and earn for us the gift of Heaven.

He passionately desires to dwell in the crib of our hearts. After his Ascension he sent the Holy Spirit to enable us to call Jesus "Lord" and to love as he loved more fully. Christians believe that Jesus's birth is the center of human history.

A poet wrote that out of love for us, the mighty God whose hands created the sun, moon, stars, and planets and hurled then into space became a tiny helpless baby. His hands were so small that they could not reach up to touch the noses of the oxen which warmed him with their hayed breath.

The Dignity of Children

In his 2006 Christmas homily, Pope Benedict XVI said that, "The child of Bethlehem directs our gaze towards all children who suffer and are abused in the world, the born and the unborn ... Towards children who are placed as soldiers in a violent world; towards children who have no bed; toward children who suffer deprivation and hunger; towards children who are unloved. Let us ask God to help us do our part so that the dignity of children may be respected. May they all experience the light of love, which mankind needs so much more than the material necessities of life."

Around Christmas sometimes we hear of homeless and lonely persons who feel they are abandoned by God, family, friends, or others. The Christmas joy of others only reminds them of loved ones who died or friends who are no longer with them. The empty chair and empty places at the dinner table make their home and heart feel empty. Unemployment and tough economic times magnify the cross of sadness for some.

Sharing God's Love

During Advent and the Christmas season, generous persons sometimes visit shut-ins and nursing home residents. Others bring food baskets to families and toys and clothes to poor children.

This year, millions of Americans and others were deeply touched but the New York policeman who gave a new pair of winter shoes to an elderly homeless man who was shivering in the cold. The man told him it was the first pair of shoes he ever had.

The policeman's generous act was a beautiful representation of the presence of Christ in the world. It was a glorious way to begin the Advent Season and prepare for Christmas. It reminded us that out of love for us, God the Father gave us Jesus, the greatest of all gifts. Jesus taught us and invited us to walk in his shoes of love.

The Christmas season begins on Christmas and ends with Jesus' Baptism. During this time, as a family we celebrate the gift of Jesus' birth. We thank God for our family and give each member the present of quality presence.

May we celebrate the Christmas season with the reverence, awe and faith expressed in the song "Silent Night." In this Year of Faith may we share God's gift of love during the Christmas season and every day.

3: Twenty Christmas Eves in Jail

I spent 20 Christmas Eves in jail. My first such Christmas Eve was in 1971. The Rock County Jail Chaplaincy Committee invited me to help to plan and participate in an ecumenical service at the jail in Janesville. I accepted.

But I waited nervously for Christmas Eve.

Nervous Anticipation

Christmas Eve finally came, and I drove anxiously to the Rock County Jail. The beautiful Christmas snowflakes that danced gracefully across my car's windshield failed to calm the nervous butterflies in my stomach.

When I arrived at the jail, I timidly identified myself to the receptionist. I felt tense. So, I prayed my favorite prayer, "Help!"

My prayer seemed answered by silence. Then some Jail Chaplaincy Committee members arrived, and the butterflies quickly flew away. "Thank you, Jesus, for answering my prayer," I whispered.

A muscular guard led us past a maze of cells to a room that was temporarily converted into our chapel. I fumbled nervously with my notes until another guard led the inmates into our makeshift chapel.

Members of the committee who were regular visitors knew some of the inmates and greeted them warmly. The services were voluntary, but most inmates attended.

"Love as He Loved"

The service began. Our musicians led us in singing Christmas carols. Carols are poems set to music. They touch us deeply because they express the inexpressible mystery of Christ's Christmas love in a deeper way than prose. Since we knew the songs, we sang them with the sincerity, if not the skill, of the angels who sang in heavenly way in the shepherd's fields near Bethlehem.

The inmates listened attentively to the proclamation of the Scripture and the preaching of Christ's Christmas message of hope and peace. We told them that Christmas is a time of giving gifts. We reminded them that the greatest Christmas present is God's gift of Jesus to us. In John 3:16 it says, "For God so loved the world that he gave his only Son so that everyone who believes in him might not perish but might have eternal life."

Jesus died on the cross to redeem us from sin and offer us the gift of heaven. Jesus became like us so we could become like him. He modeled for us how to live a Christ-like life. After his ascension, he sent the Holy Spirit to empower us to love as he loved.

We told the inmates that, like them, Jesus was a prisoner (of Pontius Pilate). But, unlike them, Jesus was innocent. From the cross where he died for our sins, Jesus offered paradise to the repentant thief who confessed his sin. The good thief repented and was saved.

Thanksgiving for Blessings

The prisoners joined us in offering prayers for family, friends, and others in need. We praised and thanked God for our blessings.

Our musicians closed the service by leading us in another inspiring Christmas carol. After the service ended, we gave fruit, candy, and cards to inmates. The inmates thanked us for sharing Christmas with them and for the presents that our committee shared with their families.

During the service I was deeply touched by the Bible passage from Matthew 25:36, "I was in prison and you visited me."

I felt that I was at Bethlehem's stable with fellow shepherds. Mary and Joseph were also there. I felt a bond with inmates, guards, and captive congregation. The prisoners taught me that "There but for God's grace go I." They also helped me to realize that we often live in prisons of violence, selfishness, and sin. Jesus will free us from this prison if we let him.

They Don't Walk Alone

I pray that, when they pay their debt to society, the inmates will continue their journey of faith and become responsible productive citizens. Some days their journey will be difficult. They will need our prayers and support. Like us, they must believe that they don't walk alone. Jesus walks with them and will help them.

Another Christmas Eve I enjoyed the privilege of celebrating Mass at Oakhill Correctional Institute near Oregon. In my homily I told the inmates that I knew they would rather be somewhere else.

But there was no place I would rather be on Christmas Eve than there, celebrating Mass with them.

I told them to trust in Jesus. He will give them the strength and courage to carry their cross when they become weary or discouraged. Since then, I moved and am presently not able to participate in jail services.

The Christmas Eves that I spent in jail were God's special Christmas gifts to me. I received more than I gave. Let us pray that prison inmates have a blessed Christmas and celebrate next Christmas Eve with their families. May their Christmas Eves and yours be as blessed as mine.

4: Christmas Peace – A Gift for Jesus and the World

A few years ago, playwright/director Peter Rothstein created a theatrical concert and musical radio drama entitled, All is Calm: The Christmas Truce of 1914. This theatrical concert dramatizes a remarkable incident of peace that happened during an unplanned truce during World War I, which some called the war to end all wars.

A Christmas Truce

On Christmas Eve, at certain places along the front, German and British soldiers spontaneously sang Christmas carols. On Christmas day unarmed enemy soldiers met in no man's land, and exchanged gifts of tobacco, rum, chocolate, and even family photographs. In one section they buried each other's dead and played soccer.

In some areas the truce continued the next day. But the high command of both armies quickly ordered that further "informal misunderstandings" with the enemy would be severely punished. Peace ended and the bloody war resumed for another four years.

The estimated number of casualties in World War I exceeded those of any other war before World War II. But this Christmas truce fulfilled briefly Jesus' dream to bring peace on earth and good will to all. It showed us the deep longing of human hearts for peace.

War is Not the Will of God

At Christmas, we celebrate the birth of Jesus, the Prince of Peace. In Luke 2:11-14 the angel says, "For today in the city of David, a savior has been born for you who is Messiah and Lord. And this will be a sign for you. You will find an infant wrapped in swaddling clothes and lying in a manger. And suddenly there was a multitude of the heavenly host with the angel praising God and saying, 'Glory to God in the highest and on earth peace on whom his favor rests.'"

Jesus fulfilled Old Testament prophecies of a messiah of peace. He redeemed us from our sins and taught us how to live in peace as a family. He taught us to respond to violence by turning the other cheek, going the extra mile, and forgiving enemies. In Matthew 26:52, Jesus tells Peter to put away his sword for violence begets more violence.

We Cannot Achieve Peace Alone

The Church led by the pope and bishops continues Christ's work for peace. In No. 168 of the Pacem in Terris, Blessed Pope John XXIII wrote, "So magnificent is this aim (for peace) that human resources alone, even though inspired by the most praiseworthy good will, cannot hope to achieve it. God must come to man's aid with his heavenly assistance if human society is to bear the closest possible resemblance to the kingdom of God."

And God will, if we ask. God began the process of peace by sending us his son.

In his 2007 World Day of Peace Message, Pope Benedict XVI stated that peace is not only a divine "gift" but also a human "task." In his 2006 Christmas homily, Pope Benedict XVI urged the world to love children more and wished peace for our world. He stressed that we must protect children who are abused, forced to bed, and are unloved.

At the age of 93, Pablo Casals, the great cellist wrote, "We live in an age in which men have accomplished magnificent things and made marvelous advances. Yet like barbarians, we fear our neighbors on earth. We arm against them and they arm against us. This must be halted if we are to survive. A brotherhood among all men must be recognized if life is to remain."

At age 84, Pablo promoted peace and brotherhood by performing his oratorio, "The Manger" all over the world. He explained, "My contribution to peace may be small. But as least I will have given all I can to an ideal I hold sacred."

Reject Hatred for Sake of Others

Peace begins when we respect each other as uniquely created in God's image. Once we lose respect for others and treat them as objects, the door to violence opens. Reverence for life diminishes when we accept any form of violence as commonplace. To achieve peace, we must reject hatreds that lead to personal conflicts and bigger wars. We must also work to eliminate poverty, injustice, and deprivation of human rights that prepare hearts for war.

Christ embraced a human nature so he could teach us how to live as families of peace. In peaceful families we learn to treat each other with reverence, love, and forgiveness. We respond to difficult situations in non-violent, peaceful ways.

Christ was born to bring peace and good will to all. Christmas invites us to disarm our hearts of sinful violence and make room for Jesus to fill them with peace. Then we do our part to help Christ's dream of peace come true and enjoy a peaceful Christmas and New Year in our homes, in our community and our world. This is one of the best presents we can offer Jesus and the world.

5: Donna Showed Me the Meaning of Christmas Love

I especially remember the Christmas when Donna taught me that Christmas is about love. We were a family of five children plus Mom and Dad.

Donna, my seven-year-old sister with a generous heart, wanted to buy a present for every member of our family. This was an ambitious undertaking for a little girl because our family was poor.

Donna Launches Her Project

This meant buying six presents. Undaunted and inspired by love, Donna launched her ambitious project. Mom, relatives, and friends helped by manufacturing odd jobs for her. She saved her pennies and nickels. In those days, nickels were like quarters today.

One by one the presents miraculously appeared under the tree. I quickly spotted mine! It looked like a box of BBs; the kind we boys sometimes shot at windows.

But, filled with the Christmas spirit, Donna was so happy that my greed-o-meter kicked in. I rationalized that no one could be that happy over a mere box of BBs. I surely deserved more than that. On Christmas, I discovered that my Christmas present was just a box of BBs. I was disappointed. "Is this all I get?" I grumbled angrily.

My ingratitude hurt Donna's feelings. She began to cry. Donna had the spirit of true Christmas love. I did not! I was the Grinch who tried to steal Christmas.

God Gives His Son to Us

In John 3:16 it says, "Yes, God so loved the world that God gave us his only Son, that whoever believes in him may not die, but may have eternal life." God loved us so much that he sent his son Jesus, who became like us so we could become more like him.

Christ Models Love for Us

When Christ the Word became flesh, he modeled for us how to love by going the extra mile, turning the other cheek, forgiving seven times seven, and dying on the cross to redeem us from sin. When Jesus returned to the Father, he sent the Holy Spirit to empower us to love as he loved.

Since Christmas brings families together, we can respond to God's gift of Christmas love by worshipping as a family and by thanking God for the blessings of family, friends, Jesus, and the "Donnas" in our life. We can make ourselves more present to the presence of God and family. Parents can take their children to the crib and tell them that Jesus was born to bring peace to the human family and our family. Christmas is truly a feast of love.

Truly Celebrating Christmas

The spirit of Christmas can inspire us to write, call, or pray for a forgotten, hurting, or lonely person. It can motivate us to remember our service men and women and those who are homeless. Christmas can move us to do a loving deed in the parish, family, or workplace.

To truly celebrate Christmas, we must receive Christ in the crib of our heart so that through the Holy Spirit Christ graces us to love as he did.

May our Christmas be filled with the joyful giving of Donna – who reflected the love of Jesus, Mary, Joseph and the angel's joyous song of peace. Let's pray and work for peace on earth and good will to all during the New Year. May we receive the love of Jesus so we can enrich the world with embraces of Christmas peace and love.

6: The Lasting Spirit of Christmas

During World War II near London, on Christmas morning, some lonely American soldiers looked for a mass to celebrate the birth of Jesus. As they searched, they discovered an old gray stone building. Carved over the door were the words, "Queen Anne's Orphanage." They knocked and a matron came to the door. She explained that the children were orphans whose parents had been killed in bombing raids.

Sharing the Christmas Spirit

The soldiers went inside as the children tumbled happily out of bed and hurried into the gray guest room. There were no Christmas trees, crib, or presents. The soldiers wished the children "Merry Christmas" and gave them whatever gifts they found in their pockets. These included a stick of chewing gum, a lifesaver, a nickel, a dime, a pencil, a pocketknife, and a yo-yo.

One soldier noticed a little boy, alone in the corner. He looked like his nephew. So, he asked him, "Big guy, what do you want for Christmas?" The boy replied, "Could you please hold me?" With tears flooding his face, the compassionate soldier picked up the boy and held him close to his heart. They gave each other "Christmas."

Christ Unites Himself with Man

On Christmas, God reached down and embraced the human race with the gift of Jesus. In John 3:16 it says, "Yes, God so loved the world that he gave his only Son, that whoever believes in him may not die, but may have eternal life." The birth of Christ is the center of human history. This is why we date history B. C. and A. D.

God Created us In the Divine Image

We imagine God best when we love because God is love. Selfishness, hatred, murder, resentment, and other sins weaken our ability to love.

God gave us Jesus to redeem us from sin and show us how to love. Christ died for our sins, rose, and sent the Holy Spirit to enable us to call him "Lord." God became like us so we could become like him and help to bring about the kingdom. To do this, we must receive God in the crib of our heart.

Celebrate the Christmas Season

We must remember that the Christmas season lasts beyond Christmas. Twice on December 26 I tried to buy recordings of Christmas songs that included "We Three Kings." The store clerks told me the tapes were sent back because Christmas was over. However, according to the Ordo of the Catholic church, this year the Christmas season extends from evening Prayer I of Christmas through the Baptism of the Lord on January 9, 2011. Some years the Christmas season lasts longer.

During the Christmas season, we celebrate feasts that remind us that Christ was born into a family. These feasts include the Holy Family, the Solemnity of Mary, the Mother of God, and Epiphany.

We can fruitfully celebrate the Christmas season by reading the Bible or other spiritual reading in prayerful silence. We can pass on Christ's Christmas love by caroling, volunteer work, or giving to the needy. We can remember that there are lonely persons whom we can call, write, or visit. These actions show that our faith is not just a warm glow at Christmas but a way of following Jesus.

Jesus Is the Bread of Life

At Christmas as we receive communion, we can recall that Mary placed the infant Jesus in a manger, a feedbox for animals. She reminds us that Jesus is the Bread of Life. He wants to come into the home of our heart and offer us eternal life.

We receive communion to unite our hearts with Jesus and to strengthen us to be Christ to others. May the spirit of Christmas help us to brighten hearts every day, everywhere.

7: A Time to make and Keep Resolutions

A small business manager asked employees who wished to write out their New Year's resolutions. He promised to post them by lunchtime on the bulletin board as it sounded like fun. When the resolutions were posted, the employees gathered eagerly around the bulletin board. Suddenly, one employee began to complain angrily to everyone there that her resolution wasn't posted. She griped that she felt left out again.

The manager sprinted quickly to his office and discovered her resolution in a pile of clutter. He glanced at her resolution, apologized to her, and asked if she wanted her resolution posted.

"Isn't that what I'm complaining about?" she replied icily.

"Why don't you post your resolution instead of me, so it gets done right," he responded with a smile.

I don't know if she posted her resolution because it was "not to become angry over trivial things!" I hope she did but doing so would have required heroic humility.

Helping Us Grow

New Year's is a time to look back on the past year and to look ahead by making New Year's resolutions that, if kept, help us and others grow as persons.

One resolution might be to try to deepen our relationship with Jesus through prayer, spiritual reading, and learning more about the Mass so that we can participate in it more fully, actively, consciously, and devoutly.

Another resolution might be to work for peace. We can be peacemakers in our home, neighborhood, church, workplace, or wherever we are. Because of the violence in today's world, we can and should urge our elected representatives to work for a responsible peace. In Matthew's beatitudes, it says, "Blessed are the peacemakers for they shall be called children of God."

Another resolution might be to appreciate the blessings we have not taken for granted rather than dwelling constantly upon things we don't have. We can also thank more often those who help us.

We can resolve not to hold grudges or resentments whose damages double when we dwell on them. Doing so hurts us as much or more than the person who wronged us. We can also resolve to put people before things as Jesus taught us.

We can resolve to affirm others more often, visit someone in a nursing home or resist temptation to pass on gossip. We can deepen our active concerns for the poor.

Another resolution might be to cultivate our sense of humor but never at the expense of others. Healthy humor helps us from taking ourselves too seriously. Conrad Hyers wrote, "Satan fell because of the gravity of his weight." Healthy humor helps us to stay serious or focused on doing good.

Seeking Advice

If we have the courage to ask, a spouse, parent, sibling, friend for the Holy Spirit might help us choose other resolutions.

When his father called on the phone, a son asked, "dad, what's your New Year's resolution?" he replied, "To make your mother as happy as I can all year." When his Mom took her turn on the phone, he asked her the same question. She replied, "to see that your dad keeps his New Year's resolution."

May the Lord bless you and keep you. May the Lord with his face shine upon you and be gracious to you. May the Lord look upon you kindly and give you peace! (Numbers 6:22-27)

May we help each other enjoy a happy, peaceful new year. May we help to make someone's world a bit better.

8: Jesus' Mother Inspires Us to Work for Peace

We Catholics begin the new year by celebrating the solemnity of Mary, the Mother of God. On New Year's we also celebrate the World Day of Peace. This is a feast established by Pope Paul VI and supported by other modern Popes.

In many ways, these two feasts complement each other because peace begins in the family. Responsible parents teach us to be persons of peace. Mary is Queen of Peace and the mother of the Prince of Peace.

Since New Year's is a time of new beginnings, we begin the new year by making resolutions to begin again. In this article, I suggest three resolutions.

Make Our Work A Prayer

Since we spend much time at work, a New Year's resolution might involve our work. Mary, Joseph, and Jesus can inspire us to make our work a prayer and offer it to God the Father.

We can evaluate whether we are giving an honest day's work, have a Christ-like attitude toward fellow workers, and whether our work helps to make our world a better place. Feeling that our work is worthwhile, receiving just compensation, and making our work a prayer helps us to do quality work.

St. Benedict said, "To work is to pray!" Brother Lawrence offered his work to God as prayer. We can also pray for our employers, employees, and co-workers – especially those who bear heavy burdens – and visit them if they are hospitalized. We can pray for the unemployed or help the unemployed to find work.

One of my favorite drawings of Mary is a picture of her sweeping her Nazareth home. This picture was drawn for me by an inmate at the Oregon Correctional Center. As I clean my apartment, her picture inspires me, but sometimes I wish that she were here to help me.

Foster Peace

A second New Year's resolution is to foster peace. According to the June 1988 issue of *Today in the Word*, 3,530 years of recorded world history, only 286 years saw peace. More than 8,000 peace treaties have been made and broken during this time.

The message of Pope Francis for the 2014 World Day of Peace is "Fraternity, the Foundation and Pathway to Peace." Since the beginning of his papacy, Pope Francis has stressed the need for fraternity on a local and world level. He believes that today's self-centered culture has caused many to lose their sense of responsibility and fraternal relationships.

Often the poor and needy are seen as burdens rather than brothers and sisters called to share the gifts of creation. To combat our throw away culture, he stresses the need for a culture of order to build a more just and peaceful world.

In John 14:27, Jesus says, "Peace I leave with you. My peace I give you. Not as the world gives do I give it to you." The peace of Jesus is not just a peace characterized by absence of conflict or a ceasefire. It is characterized by respect and harmony in our relationship with God and others.

Do God's Will

The third resolution is to try harder to do God's will as Mary did. Certainly, God's will is to keep the commandments and to live the Gospel.

Specifically, God's will is to be peaceful and Christ-like in personal challenging situations. Reflecting upon and praying the prayer of St. Francis helps us to work for peace in our family, workplace, city, nation, and world. Pope John XXIII said that we can only achieve peace with God's help.

A good New Year's resolution is to pray this prayer daily and ask the Holy Spirit for courage and wisdom to live this prayer:

> Lord, make me an instrument of your peace.
> Where there is hatred, let me sow love;
> Where there is injury, pardon;
> Where there is doubt, faith;
> Where there is despair, hope;
> Where there is darkness, light;
> And Where there is sadness, joy;
> Oh Divine Master, grant that I may not so much
> Seek to be consoled as to console;
> To be understood as to understand;
> To be loved as to love.
> For it is in giving that we receive;
> It is in pardoning that we are pardoned;
> And it is in dying that we are born to eternal life.
> Amen joy.

III: ORDINARY TIME

Chapter One: Pro-Life

1: Be a part of the Pro-Life Cause to End Abortion

In his visit to the United States, Pope Francis especially praised two Catholics. They were Thomas Merton and Dorothy Day.

In 1925, Dorothy Day became pregnant. Because of a previous abortion, her pregnancy seemed a miracle. She had to make the toughest decision she ever made. If she gave birth, Forster Batterham, the child's father, would leave her. He would stay with her if she aborted their baby.

On March 4, 1926, Dorothy gave birth to Tamar Teresa. She had Tamar baptized and raised her as a Catholic. Later, Dorothy became a Catholic. Her decisions caused her to lose the man she thought she loved. But she gained salvation for herself and Tamar.

After her conversion, Dorothy married Peter Maurin. Together, they founded the Catholic Worker movement which works on behalf of the poor and homeless. She became a zealous Catholic. For the rest of her life, she regretted the abortion of her first baby. She pleaded with others not to have abortions because of its devastating effects, which she personally experienced.

It's normal for a woman to grieve a pregnancy loss by abortion or miscarriage. Aborting a baby can form a hole so deep in her heart that sometimes it seems nothing can fill the emptiness. It can also affect fathers of children lost to abortion, grandparents, other relatives, health care providers, and many others.

Secular humanism helps to create a climate that makes abortion more acceptable as evidenced by the Roe v. Wade Supreme Court decision. On January 22, 1973, the United States Supreme Court legalized abortion in the Roe v. Wade decision.

What We Can Do

We can help the pro-life cause in many ways as Pope Francis urges. We can participate in the 40-day Pro-Life Vigil in Madison, which consists of 40 days of prayer, fasting, and witness by volunteer pro-lifers.

We can pray for or spiritually adopt unborn babies. We can cooperate with others who oppose abortion and urge our elected representatives to support legislation that protects the unborn and support a human life amendment. We can donate to pro-life causes.

We can tell women, and men, who grieve from an abortion about Project Rachel.

Project Rachel is a post-abortion healing ministry. It was founded in 1984 in the Milwaukee Archdiocese by Vicki Thorn. Project Rachel's mission is to provide a confidential and compassionate ministry that offers resources for spiritual, emotional, and psychological healing to anyone who has been impacted by abortion regardless of faith background.

As Catholics we must respect life, not only in the womb, but everywhere, within our families, our communities, and where we work or do business.

This means treating every life with dignity and honoring every life as God's gift. We Catholics should faithfully involve ourselves as advocates for the weak and marginalized. Catholic public officials are obliged to address each of the issues the American bishops listed in Living the Gospel of Life as they seek to build consistent policies which promote respect for human persons at all stages of life.

2: Ultrasound Images Provide a Window to the Womb

On January 22, 1973, the United States Supreme Court legalized abortion in the Roe v. Wade decision. Justice Byron White who dissented stated, "The court apparently values the convenience of a pregnant mother more than the continued existence and development of the life or potential life she carries."

Since Roe v. Wade, 58 million abortions have occurred in our country. This is roughly the population of the United States around 1869. The Catholic Church teaches that human life begins at conception. When a woman becomes pregnant, and doesn't want their baby, she may be embarrassed, frightened, and confused. She may consider abortion. Some friends may suggest she get an abortion.

Pro-Life Pregnancy Centers

Others may encourage her to visit a pro-life pregnancy center. In the Diocese of Madison, pro-life pregnancy clinics include Platteville's Clarity Clinic, Madison's Women's Care Center, and Beloit's Stateline Pregnancy Center. These clinics offer free pregnancy tests, free ultrasounds, and confidentiality which often attracts struggling low-income expectant mothers considering abortion.

When a pregnant woman visits one of these centers, the pro-life counselor who believes that the woman is carrying an unborn baby in her womb encourages her to give birth. Then the woman, hopefully supported by the father, decides to raise the child or offer him or her for adoption.

Importance of Ultrasound

Pro-life counselors are optimistic about the importance of ultrasound images in the decision process. In 1983, two government researchers published an article in the *New England Journal of Medicine* about pregnant women who underwent ultrasound tests while considering abortions.

Viewing the unborn children early in pregnancy, before movement is felt by the mother, may "influence the resolution of any ambivalence toward the pregnancy itself in favor of the fetus," wrote Drs. John C. Fletcher, then of the National Institutes of Health, and Mark I. Evans, then of George Washington University Medical School. Ultrasound examination may thus result in fewer abortions and more desired pregnancies.

Drs. Fletcher and Evans wrote that one woman who was beaten early in pregnancy was given the ultrasound test to see whether her child had been injured in the womb. When she saw her child's image moving on the screen, she said, "I feel that it is human. It belongs to me. I couldn't have an abortion now."

Need Financial Support

Financial support is needed to help support pro-life pregnancy centers. The National Institute of Family and Life Advocates hopes to help equip one-third of our nation's pregnancy centers with ultrasound machines and trained staff.

On January 22, 2009, the Knights of Columbus launched an

ultrasound initiative. As of June of 2014, numerous local and state councils have qualified for matching funds from the Supreme Council office towards the purchase of over 460 ultrasound machines at a cost of over $13.5 million.

Beloit's Knights of Columbus Council 605 and South Beloit's Knights of Columbus Council 8021 helped to purchase an ultrasound machine for the Stateline Pregnancy Center which serves Illinois and Wisconsin. Ultrasound machines along with increased support to mothers offer hope for unborn babies.

3: Respect All Human Life, Especially the Unborn

Respect Life Month in October invites us to respect life across the board. We should especially respect and defend the rights of helpless unborn babies who cannot defend themselves. The 2016 Doritos Super Bowl commercial showed an unborn baby in his or her mother's womb. To me, this was natural and obvious. I was familiar with advances in ultrasound imaging and I think that human life begins at conception as the Church teaches.

Life in the Womb Can't Be Denied

I didn't expect it, but I wasn't surprised by comments from some affiliated with the National Abortion Rights Action League (NARAL) who criticized Doritos for "humanizing fetuses." Cal Thomas of the Tribune Content Agency responded, "Humanizing fetuses? What does that sonogram image show if not a human?" He added, "Pro-choice persons fear the sonogram because it shows an image whose humanness cannot be denied."

Ironically, as abortion became more common after being legalized in Roe v. Wade, knowledge about life within the womb increased. Advancements in ultrasound imaging reveal three-dimensional images of unborn babies as the Doritos' commercial did. Expectant mothers are discouraged from smoking, taking drugs, or drinking alcohol. Expectant parents are encouraged to interact with their unborn child through talking and music.

Clear Catholic Teaching

In No. 2271 of the Catechism of the Catholic Church, it says, "Since the first century, the Church has affirmed the moral evil of every procured abortion. This teaching has not changed and remains unchangeable."

On September 20, 2013, in a talk to a group of Catholic doctors, Pope Francis condemned the "throwaway culture" abortion promotes. He stated, "Every unborn child, though unjustly condemned to be aborted, has the face of Jesus, who before his birth, and shortly after he was born, experienced the world's rejection."

Supporting the Right to Life of the Unborn

Statistics reveal that abortions have decreased slightly in recent years, but there are still too many abortions. We must keep supporting the right to life of the unborn. We can tell others about pro-life ministries that work with expectant mothers considering abortion and encourage them to choose life for their unborn children. Pro-life ministries provide pre-natal care, assistance in raising children, adoption placement services, and much more.

We can tell women who grieve from having an abortion about Project Rachel, which helps them heal through counseling, prayer, and forgiveness. We can participate in 40 Days for Life and pray for or spiritually adopt unborn babies. As Catholics we must respect life, not only in the womb, but everywhere, within our families, our communities, and where we work or do business. This means treating every life with dignity and honoring every life as God's gift.

4: Let Us Continue to Speak for the Unborn

Have you ever seen a speaker weep when giving a talk on abortion? I have. When I taught high school religion, a pro-life doctor gave a talk to my classes. As he described the tragedy of aborted babies, he wept. His tears convinced me that he truly believed that unborn babies were human persons and aborting them destroyed human life.

There were trails of tears in the hearts and eyes of committed pro-lifers when on January 22, 1973, in the Roe v. Wade decision when the Supreme Court legalized abortion. Their ruling made it legal for the mother, sometimes encouraged by the father, to abort their unborn baby.

According to Dr. Ronda Chervin, in 1925 Whitakker Chambers became a member of the Communist party, partially because he thought Communists were genuinely concerned for the poor. He began working for the party in minor ways, and then as a newspaper editor in NYC. He married a woman who was not a Communist, but an anarchist. Abortion was common in the party because many believed that it was a crime to bring children into such an evil world. When Chamber's wife got pregnant, he was joyful but still thought she should have an abortion. She said, "We could not do that awful thing to a little baby." It was through this child that he found God in this way: "My daughter was in her highchair. I was watching her eat. She was the most miraculous thing that had ever happened in my life. I liked to watch her even when she smeared porridge on her face or dropped it meditatively on the floor. My eyes came to rest on the delicate convolutions of her ear – those intricate, perfect ears. The thought passed through my mind: 'No, those ears were not created by any chance coming together of atoms in nature (the Communist view). They could have been created only by immense design.' The thought was involuntary and unwanted. I crowded it out of my mind. But I never wholly forgot it or the occasion. I had to crowd it out of my mind. If I had completed it, I should have had to say: Design presupposes God. I did not then know that, at that moment, the finger of God was first laid upon my forehead.

This experience eventually led him to believe in God, in God's importance and the natural law.

On June 28, 2018, Pope Francis said respect for life begins at conception and begins through childhood, adolescence, adulthood, old age, as well as those moments of life web it is fragile, and sick, wounded, offended and demoralized.

Gianna Jessen, a popular prolife speaker was the victim of a failed saline abortion at seven and a half months' gestation. She was rushed from the clinic to the hospital, doctors said she wouldn't live. But she did. The doctors also said she would never walk or even hold up her own head. But she began walking at three and has grown into a woman who has run marathons and has become a pro-life advocate, speaker, singer, and writer.

In our culture there is often a battle between objective and subjective morality. This clash doesn't occur on battlefields, but in legislatures, courtrooms, schools, churches, workplaces, neighborhoods, and consciences.

We can support life in this battle by urging elected representatives to support legislation that protects the unborn and by supporting a human life amendment.

As Catholics we must respect life, not only in the womb, but everywhere, within our families, our communities, and where we work or do business.

This means treating every life with dignity and honoring every life as God's gift. We Catholics should faithfully involve ourselves as advocates for the weak and marginalized. Catholic public officials are obliged to address each of the issues the American bishops listed in Living the Gospel of Life, as they seek to build consistent policies which promote respect for human persons at all stages of life.

We can also participate in the 40-day Pro-Life Vigil in Madison, which consists of 40 days of prayer, fasting, and witness by volunteer pro-lifers. Our parish, diocese, Catholic newspaper, and the Holy Spirit invite us to support the pro-life cause in other ways, Pope John Paul II stressed that children are the hope of the future. However, if their lives are snuffed out in the womb, unborn children have no earthly future. Since they cannot speak for themselves, we must defend their God given right to be born. The battle for the rights of the unborn will be long and hard. But the unborn who cannot speak for themselves are worth it.

We can also pray this prayer, written by the Venerable Fulton J. Sheen, or other prayers for an end to abortion and increased respect for life: "Jesus, Mary and Joseph, I love you very much. I beg you to spare the life of the [baby's name/unborn child] that I have spiritually adopted who is in danger of abortion."

Chapter Two: Vocations

1: Annual Priests Assembly Offers Special Graces

A special grace of my priesthood is the privilege of participating in the annual Diocesan Presbyterial Assembly held at Chula Vista

Resort in Wisconsin Dells from September 21 to 24 this year.

The Presbyterial Assembly grew out of the landmark Madison Diocese Emmaus retreat in 1980, which was intended to bolster the spiritual lives of us priests. It did.

Since I was in high school work at Beloit Catholic High, for twenty years I rarely was able to attend diocesan functions, but I was free during summers. During summer school, I learned that this was also true of priests who taught high school in other dioceses. I was happy that Bishop Cletus F. O'Donnell asked all active priests to attend.

Emmaus Experience

Msgr. Frank Bognanno of the Diocese of Des Moines was chosen to lead the Emmaus retreat. The bishop of Des Moines was Bishop Bullock, who later became our bishop. Father Frank returned to Madison for Bishop Bullock's anniversary celebration. He also led an inspiring priests' retreat in 2000.

The Emmaus retreat was based on Luke 24:13-35. The Risen Jesus walked with two unnamed disciples on the road to Emmaus, but they didn't recognize him. With sadness, they discussed what happened to Jesus and what might happen to them and the early Church. Then Jesus revealed himself in the "Breaking of the Bread" or the Eucharist. Christ also calls us to walk with him and longs to reveal himself to us in the Eucharist.

Emmaus reflection groups grew out of the Emmaus retreat. These groups consisted of five to seven or more priests who met monthly. I was in a group with Fr. Richard Lenarz and Fr. Albert Schubiger of Beloit and other priests.

The format or practice among several priest groups was to select a meeting date with an overnight so that after a good night's rest the priests were ready to pray, share their faith, pastoral experiences, and dialogue about how they might grow in their spiritual lives. The results were positive and benefited our diocese.

Annual Priests' Assembly

The priests' assembly originally lasted a day and a half. In 1993, it was extended from Sunday evening to Wednesday at noon. It is a time when priests of the diocese gather for prayer, instruction, dialogue on a current topic, and enjoy each other's company. The bishop also speaks on diocesan and other important matters. He invites all active priests to attend and retired priests who desire and are able to attend.

Topics are selected, and presenters are recruited by a planning committee and the Office for the Continuing Education of Priests headed by Msgr. Charles Schluter. This office also helps plan the annual priests' retreat. We priests benefit from their creativity and commitment.

During my drive to the priests' assembly, generally there is a Packers game or other football game that I listen to on the radio. If I lose radio reception, I can usually tell if the Packers won or lost by the smile or frown on faces of Packer priests when I arrive.

Praying for the Deceased

A moving part of the priests' assembly, which brings tears to many eyes, is when we pray for deceased priests, bishops of the diocese, and popes. As each name is read, priests and bishops present realize that someday their name will be read.

After a certain number of names are read, we sing the very singable moving prayer, "Jesus, remember me when you come into your kingdom." In doing so, we express our hope that our departed priests, bishops, and popes enjoy the gift of the fullness of eternal life.

The theme and focus of this year's Priests Assembly XXXIV is "Reflecting on the Sacred Liturgy." Fr. Douglas Martis will be the presenter. He is the director of the Liturgical Institute and chair of the Department of Systematic and Department of Worship at Mundelein Seminary. We priests are always eager to learn more about the sacred liturgy because it is crucial to serving Catholics as a priest.

A banquet honoring priests who celebrate a priestly anniversary is held on Tuesday evening. The priests honored share many memorable personal, spiritual, and sometimes humorous stories of their priestly ministry.

Health of Priests

If I recall correctly, some priorities that came out of the original Emmaus retreat were the physical, mental, and spiritual health of priests. In his book, Habits of a Priestly Heart, Fr. Eugene Hemrick, director of the National Institute for the Renewal of the Priesthood, stresses that these and other qualities are needed by today's priests, Religious, and laity.

Please continue to pray for all priests, but especially for us who attend the Presbyterial Assembly from September 21 to 24, so that we come back ready to serve with renewed energy and Christ-like enthusiasm.

2: I Thank God for Calling Me to be a Priest

We celebrate Vocation Awareness week from January 10 to 16, 2010. I believe that priests, deacons, and religious can help Catholics to become more aware of vocations when they share their story. With this hope, I share these reflections on my journey to priesthood.

In this Year of the Priest, I thank God for calling me to serve as a priest for nearly 40 years, I am the luckiest person on the face of God's good earth.

God planted the seeds of my call to priesthood in me when I was six. Whenever I met Father Grevildinger on Kieler's Main St, I greeted him "Good morning, Father." Then I extended my hand and Father gave me pennies or nickels, I proudly told everyone I met that I wanted to become a kind priest like him. However, the seeds of God's call grew slowly in my heart's rocky soil.

In grade school the nuns, my parents, and especially Fr. Albert Goetzman, a Christ-like priest, helped to keep my desire to be a priest alive. However, after second grade I hid my desire under a bushel basket of shyness. After I graduated from grade school, I went to Loras, a Catholic high school, where I fantasized that I would star in football.

Hearing the Call

As a sophomore, I worked for a farmer and hoped to gain more weight for football. My football dreams ended when I became trapped under a powerful Case tractor. In desperation, I promised God that if I were rescued, I would go to seminary. But after being saved, I quickly forgot my promise. When a counselor asked if I was interested in priesthood, I mumbled guiltily, "No!"

In the Navy, I thought of priesthood again. But after discharge, I attended Platteville University and graduated with an English major and a teaching degree. I taught grade school for about four months in Dubuque and English for two years at New Lisbon High School in Wisconsin.

These were good years, but, at age 29, the Holy Spirit whispered that if I were to ever go to seminary, the time was now. I listened and asked my pastor to recommend me to the Sacred Heart Fathers. He suggested that I talk to our diocese first. I met with our vocational director and entered the seminary to study for the Diocese of Madison.

Work of the Holy Spirit

After two years of philosophy, I anticipated a relaxing summer. Then I would study theology. However, as autumn approached, not knowing whether I would be allowed to continue my studies for priesthood created deep stress. In August, to relax, I went swimming with my brother. As I swam the crawl, my weakest stroke, I became tired. My tiredness plus the stress caused by an increasingly uncertain future made me panic.

I sank under the water and thought I would drown. Then an inner voice whispered, "If you drown, you won't be able to be a priest. Relax, trust in God, surface, and swim the backstroke to safety." Obediently, I surfaced and swam the backstroke, my best stroke, to shore.

A remarkable number of co-incidences seemed to converge. My high school classmate, already an ordained priest, was there. My loyal brother and a student who gave me much grief tried to rescue me. Now I believe it was the work of the Holy Spirit. I was allowed to study theology and became a priest four years later.

Unique Call from God

I like being a priest. I enjoyed all my assignments. I feed fellow Catholics spiritually by administering the sacraments, presiding at Mass, preaching, and shepherding. I minister to parishioners at key spiritual moments. These include First Communions, marriages, Baptisms, anniversaries, Mass, hospital visits, and more. I pray for them and their prayers help me more than they know.

I visit the sick, bury the dead, counsel the doubtful, feed the hungry, teach the young, comfort the sorrowful, and pray for the living and dead. Like brother-priests, I sacrificed the privilege and responsibility of marriage and family. But I gained many families and friends, Catholics have been very kind and supportive of me.

As a retired priest I enjoy presiding at Mass and hearing Confessions. I thank all members of the priest's retirement ministry, the Knights of Columbus, parishes, and others who offered encouragement, support, and prayers.

A vocation is a unique call from God and a mystery of grace. Sometimes God calls the least likely persons to be priests. I am one of these. Like Lou Gehrig, a great baseball player, I feel that I am the luckiest person on the face of the earth.

If you are a single young or older man and think that God is calling you to priesthood, please talk with a priest, bishop, religion teacher, or diocesan vocation director or attend a vocation discernment weekend. God may be calling you. If so, we need you.

Chapter Three: Dr. Martin Luther King

1: Continuing to Follow Dr. King's Dream

Martin Luther King, Jr. Day is an American federal holiday that marks the birthday of Martin Luther King, Jr. It is observed on the third Monday of January which is around Dr. King's birthday, January 15. Dr. King was the chief spokesman for nonviolent activism in the Civil Rights movement which successfully protested racial discrimination in federal and state law.

I Have a Dream Speech

In his famous "I Have a Dream" speech, Dr. King chose not to directly attack America for her failings to live up to the Declaration of Independence; instead, he challenged Americans to live the ideals expressed in the declaration.

He reminded Americans of the self-evident truths stated in the preamble to the declaration when he declared, "I have a dream that someday America will rise up and live out the meaning of its creed that all men (and women) are created equal and are endowed by their creator with certain inalienable rights of life, liberty, and pursuit of happiness."

On April 4, 1968, Dr. Martin Luther King, Jr. was assassinated at the Lorraine Motel in Memphis, Tenn., presumably in hopes of silencing him. He became a martyr for the Civil Rights Movement. In front of the Lorraine Motel is a marker on which is written, "here cometh the Dreamer. Come on, let's slay him and we shall see what will become of his dreams." (Genesis 37:19-20).

Continuing Call for Conversion

The challenging inscription from Genesis was probably an invitation to us to continue to try to achieve the dream of Dr. King just as the Catholic Church continues to try to achieve the dream of Christ.

In No. 1896 of the Catechism of the Catholic Church it says, "Where sin has perverted the social climate, it is necessary to call for conversion of hearts and appeal to God's grace." Each new year invites us to rise up and live the meaning of our beautiful Catholic faith and creed in deeper ways. It invites us to continue to work for social justice which is a constitutive part of the Gospel.

It encourages us to keep supporting the rights of the unborn who cannot speak for themselves. In the May 2, 2015, issue of the Telegraph Herald, Alveda King, granddaughter of Martin Luther King, Sr., stated that respect for life is part of the Civil Rights Movement. She stated that abortion is not a civil right; rather, life is a civil right.

Like Dr. Martin Luther King, Jr., Pope Francis urges us to rise from the sin of indifference and be peacemakers in a world of increasing violence. May we support God's gifts of family and marriage and work to improve the environment by caring for Mother Earth.

Responding to these and other challenges helps us to become better Catholics and citizens. They are at the center of social justice, public life, and pursuit of the common good.

2: Inspires Us to Work for Equality

Martin Luther King, Jr. Day is an American federal holiday that marks his birthday, observed this year on January 15.

In his speech to Congress in September of 2015, Pope Francis lifted up four Americans who worked for social justice. Dorothy Day and Thomas Merton were Catholics. Abraham Lincoln and Rev. Dr. Martin Luther King, Jr. were not Catholics.

Dr. King was the chief spokesman for nonviolent activism in the

Civil Rights Movement which successfully protested racial discrimination in federal and state law.

The campaign for a federal holiday honoring Dr. King began soon after his assassination in 1968. President Ronald Reagan signed the holiday into law in 1983. It was first observed three years later. It was officially observed in all 50 states in 2000.

"I Have A Dream" Speech

In his famous "I Have a Dream" speech, Dr. King chose not to directly attack America for her failings to live out the Declaration of Independence; instead, he challenged Americans to live out the self-evident truths expressed in the Declaration.

In his speech he declared, "I have a dream that someday America will rise up and live out the meaning of its creed that all men (and women) are created equal and are endowed by their creator with certain inalienable rights of life, liberty, and pursuit of happiness."

Inequality in America

For years, Americans tolerated legalized slavery. To abolish slavery, a bloody civil war was fought. Even after the emancipation of slaves, African Americans were often denied their rights through unjust laws, customs, and policies. Protest against these laws, practices, and customs led to the Civil Rights Movement.

On April 4, 1968, Dr. King was assassinated at the Lorraine Motel in Memphis, Tenn., presumably in hopes of silencing him.

Equality in Schools

Part of Dr. King's dream was for equality in public education. In the Plessy v. Ferguson decision in 1896, the U. S. Supreme Court established as law separate but equal facilities for black and white students in public schools.

In 1954, in the Brown v. Board of Education decision, the U. S. Supreme Court stated that separate but equal facilities are inherently unequal. The unanimous (9-0) decision declared that state laws establishing separate public schools for black and white students were unconstitutional.

On December 15, 1956, in an address to the National Committee for Rural Schools Dr. King reflected on the importance of the decision saying, "To all men of good will, this decision came as a joyous daybreak to end the long night of human captivity."

To me, the decision somewhat reflects Galatians 3:26-28, "For through faith, you are all children of God in Christ Jesus. For all of you who were baptized into Christ have clothed yourself in Christ. In Christ, there is neither Jew nor Greek, there is neither slave nor free person, there is neither male nor female, for we are all one in Christ Jesus."

Although the decision's mandate to dismantle segregated public schools initially faced massive resistance across the South, the ruling provided irresistible moral authority to the drive for legal equality that culminated in the passage of the Civil Rights and Voting Rights Acts a decade later.

Challenges Remain

Challenges to implementing Brown v. Board of Education remain, but tremendous progress has been made. These challenges add greater urgency to implementing the decision's broader goal of ensuring all young people the opportunity to develop their talents.

Each new year invites us to live out the meaning of our beautiful Catholic faith in deeper ways in our home, community, and country. Let us pray for the courage and perseverance to continue to work for social justice and quality as Dr. King and countless others have done.

Chapter Four: Unity

1: Praying and Working for Christian Unity

The Week of Prayer for Christian unity is celebrated every year from January 18-25.

Its theme for 2014 was "Has Christ Been Divided?" This theme is based upon 1 Corinthians 1:10-17, where St. Paul – angry over divisions in the Corinthian Church – wrote, "Each of you is saying 'I belong to Paul' or 'I belong to Apollos' or 'I belong to Kephas' or 'I belong to Christ.' Is Christ divided?"

In John 17:20-21 Jesus prays for unity among his followers by saying, "I pray also for those who will believe in me, so they may all be one as you Father are in me and I in you, so that the world may know that you have sent me."

Christ wants us to pray for unity within the Catholic Church. But the Week of Prayer for Christian Unity focuses upon praying for unity between churches of different denominations because Christ wanted his followers to be united.

Lack of unity hurts the holy cause of proclaiming the Gospel and witnessing to Christ.

Ecumenical Efforts

"Ecumenism" refers to movements intended to achieve greater cooperation and unity among Christian churches.

On one level of ecumenism, the churches work for unity in doctrine. Theologians contribute an important part of this level.

Another level involves focusing upon what we Catholics have in common with other churches. These include belief in Christ's divinity, prayer, love of neighbor, helping the poor, and much more.

One of the fruits of the ecumenical movement is to enable Christians of goodwill to cooperate in areas in which they agree. Churches can also work together ecumenically to counteract atheistic secular values. Today we swim and risk drowning in dangerous currents of secular values.

Activities at the Local Level

I served my first year of priesthood at St. William Parish in Janesville. At that time, most West side churches participated in ecumenism. We met as clergy, but clergy and laity also participated in "Living Room Dialogues." From these groups came the Rock County Jail Chaplaincy group and other blessings.

After a year at St. William's, I served at Beloit Catholic High for 20 years. My brief but deep involvement with ecumenism in Janesville enabled me to teach a course on ecumenism to Beloit Catholic High students.

Because I taught high school, I was free to participate with the Jail Chaplaincy group in Good Friday and Christmas Even prayer services. After the services, I could still help at St. Paul's Easter Masses and the Good Friday Service.

When I became pastor of Immaculate Conception parish in

Barneveld, we cooperated ecumenically on numerous projects with two other churches.

These projects included food pantries, working and praying for peace, cooperating with the local high school to keep "church night" sacred, and much more. After I retired, I deeply appreciated the plaque I received from Barneveld Lutheran Church.

Hope for Unity

The Graymoor Ecumenical and Interreligious Institute offers this statement of challenge and hope for unity: "Churches continue to be divided by doctrine, polity, and practice. At the same time our pilgrimage towards unity continues under God's guidance. Being faithful to Christ's desire for the Unity of his disciples has led to this year's theme which focuses on St. Paul's confronting question in 1 Corinthians: 'Has Christ Been Divided?'"

2: Ebony and Ivory Show How Music Can Unite Us

One day Margaret Patrick arrived at the Southeast Senior Center to begin physical therapy. When Mille McHugh, a staff member introduced Margaret to others, she noticed pain in Margaret's eyes as she gazed at the piano.

Millie asked, "Is there anything wrong?"

"No," Margaret responded sadly. "It's just that seeing a piano brings back memories! Before my stroke, music was everything. Now I can't play because I have only one good hand!!!"

Millie replied, "Wait here. I'll be back in a minute!"

Millie returned with a small white-haired woman wearing thick glasses. The woman used a walker.

"Margaret Patrick," said Millie, "meet Ruth Eisenberg." She too can play the piano, but like you, she's been unable to play since her stroke."

Mrs. Eisenberg has a good right hand and you have a good left hand. I have a feeling that together you could make wonderful music."

"Do you know Chopin's Waltz in D-flat?" Ruth asked.

Margaret nodded.

Then side by side, the two sat on the piano bench. Two healthy hands moved rhythmically across the ebony and ivory keys.

Since that day, they sat together over the keyboard hundreds of times. Ruth plays the melody and Margaret plays the accompaniment. Their music has moved audiences on television, churches, schools, and rehabilitation and senior citizen centers.

Both discovered that they are great-grandmothers and widows; both have lost sons, both had much to give but they discovered they couldn't give without the other's help.

Ruth heard Margaret say, "My music was taken away, but God gave me Ruth." Ruth said that it was God's miracle that brought them together. They now call themselves "Ebony and Ivory."

One sign of living a Christ-like life is helping those in need. In Acts 4:32-35 it says, "There was no needy person among them, for those who owned property or houses would sell them, bring the proceeds of the sale and put them at the apostles' feet. They were distributed to each according to their need."

A few years ago, a family lost four little children to a fire. Everyone seemed to help the grieving family in various inspiring ways. When my father died, I was moved by the way neighbors, friends, and family helped our family – digging the grave, bringing food, comfort, support, and helping them in other ways.

A 97-year-old man in assisted living told me that the place was okay but what kept him going were his three daughters who visited him regularly.

A woman was evicted because someone robbed her. She and her two girls had to spend the night in the park. As it grew darker, she watched shady looking persons drift into the park. She was scared! The next morning, she made a payphone call for help. When she returned to her daughters, she noticed a bum approached them. She was frightened.

The man apologized, "Excuse me ma'am, but I heard you talking on the phone. So, me and the fellas took up a collection to help you and your little girls. It's not much, but it may help a little." The mother began to cry as she realized that the men she mistrusted were showing her a love of which she was not capable.

If you look carefully with Jesus' eyes, you may see others share God's music of love with others.

Chapter Five: Catholic Schools Week

1: A Time to Thank Teachers

Catholic Schools Week 2013 is scheduled from January 27 to February 2. Its theme is "Catholic Schools Raise the Standards." This theme highlights the launch of a new initiative to ensure consistent high standards at Catholic schools across the country. The logo designed for this week illustrates a chart of steady growth culminating in the highest achievement of all, a cross representing the faith that underscores all Catholic education.

The Catholic Church's educational mission flows from Jesus' life and teaching. The cross symbolizes the sacrificial love that Jesus teaches us to imitate. In the Dictionary of the Bible, Fr. John L. McKenzie wrote that Jesus spent more time teaching than anything else, including working miracles, signs, and wonders. Through education, the Church continues Jesus' teaching by preparing her members to hear, live, and proclaim the Gospel. Good teachers are keys to successful Catholic schools.

In the pastoral document The Catholic School, it says, "By their witness and behavior, teachers are of first importance in imparting a distinctive character to Catholic schools." Pope Paul VI stated that modern humanity listens more willingly to witnesses than to teachers. He or she listens best to teachers who are witnesses.

Catholic Schools Week offers us graced opportunities to show appreciation for Catholic school teachers and for all teachers.

Showing Appreciation

A retreat director suggested that the retreat participants thank someone who influenced their lives. A middle-aged man remembered a teacher who helped him through a crisis in his youth. He realized that he never thanked her. After much searching, he discovered that she now resided in a nursing home. He wrote her a thank you letter.

She wrote back that she was living alone and lingering like the last leaf of summer. She added that she taught school for 50 years and his letter was the first student note of appreciation that she ever received. It came on a blue morning and cheered her as nothing had in years.

Assisting Parents

In Canon 796 of the Code of Canon Law, under Catholic Education, it says, "Among the means to foster education, the Christian faithful are to hold schools in esteem; schools are the principal assistance to parents in fulfilling the function of education."

Catholic schools offer academic subjects and extra-curricular activities. Students are guided in their learning by teachers in the basics of Catholic faith, tradition, and prayer.

Jesus revealed God's design for all creation. At its best, Catholic education sees no contradiction between true science and Christianity. Both are revelations of the same artistic creator. Whether it is a beautiful sunset described poetically, the intricate math and science laws that reveal a universe in the heavens or the mini universe of a cell, knowledge is ultimately approached with the belief that it can point to God who authored it.

Catholic education sees all knowledge as sacred especially when human insight is combined with divine revelation in the pursuit of truth, goodness, and beauty. To achieve this goal, the Church recognizes the learner's dependence on grace to bring human nature to completion.

Opportunities to Expand

Through methods appropriate to different age and learning levels, Catholic schools provide opportunities for students to explore, reflect, and integrate a Christian understanding of nature, self, society, and God. Catholic teachers, parents, and others manifest this understanding in loving lives of service.

Responsible parents lay the foundation upon which teachers in Catholic schools and religious education programs build. The Church calls parents to partnership in Catholic education's mission by taking responsibility for their own life-long learning and supporting educational opportunities offered to their children. Students also learn and reinforce Christian values from work, coaches, friends, priests, religious, and many others.

Through the minds and hearts of teachers pass future doctors, secretaries, plumbers, priests, religious, parents, singles, and workers of tomorrow. In the office of a principal whom I admired, there hung a plaque with this inspiring message, "Good teachers affect eternity. You never know where their influence stops."

Crosses Teachers Bear

During my 22 years of high school teaching, I appreciated more fully the crosses my teachers occasionally experienced. Once a former student anonymously sent me this quotation, "Our Sunday school teacher never talked down to us kids, no matter how silly we acted. I blush now to think of the outrageous questions we asked just to bait him a little. He would smile and answer us with sincerity, wisdom, and above all with patience. We in turn would learn in spite of ourselves. We loved him like a father. And he in turn taught us about the Heavenly Father. This quotation reminds me of you Father." I'm not sure he or she was right, especially regarding my patience, but I treasure the affirmation.

Catholic teachers at Immaculate Conception School in Kieler, Wisconsin, and Loras Academy in Dubuque, Iowa, taught me basics of faith, nourished my priestly vocation, and showed me how to love and serve others.

During this Year of Faith, may Catholic Schools Week inspire us to express and deepen our appreciation of Catholic Schools, especially its teachers and administrators.

2: Encourage Respect for Everyone

The Catholic school builds upon the relationship with God, knowledge, values, and community that the student experiences at home. In No. 2204 of the Catechism of the Catholic Church, it says, "the Christian family constitutes a specific revelation and realization of ecclesial communion and for this reason it can and should be called a domestic Church." Good families teach us to respect God and each other.

Build a Service Community

Catholic school students are taught faith – not just the basics of Christianity, but how to have a relationship with God. Academics help students reach their potential. Service, the giving of one's time and effort to help others, is taught both as an expression of faith and good citizenship. Knowledge and deepened faith help to build Christian community from which service flows.

When students experience Christian community, they more willingly serve their neighbor in need. As a community, faculty and students pray, receive the sacraments, participate in retreats, and worship together. Students are encouraged to respect everyone as a child of God and a graced part of a Christian community.

Need Zero Tolerance

Recently school bullying has received national attention. Bullying is an act of violence and disrespect that hurts the mission of the school. In a Catholic school everyone should be respected and loved because they are created in God's image. For this reason, there should be zero tolerance towards bullying in public and private schools. It may be good to reflect upon bullying during Catholic Schools Week.

Bullying has been a problem since Cain and Abel. However, in recent years it has received national attention and has become an emotional and physical danger from kindergarten through high school. Though technology alerts us to bullying's dangers, it also offers new avenues for it through cyber-bullying. Now youth can bully others in chat rooms or email from their homes.

Statistics of Bullying

According to the Bureau of Justice Statistics, one in four children is bullied at school. Eight percent of children miss one day of class per month because they fear bullies. Pages of evidence about the damaging effects of bullying are available on the internet and other sources.

Bullying can be verbal (making threats, name-calling), psychological (excluding children, spreading rumors), or physical (hitting, pushing, or stealing).

Grade school children sometimes bully by ridiculing the car, house, or clothes of poorer classmates. They may also call classmates cruel nicknames and exclude them from birthday parties, slumber parties, and the like. This hurts. I know. Charlie Brown said, "It's hard on a face when it gets laughed in."

Students who are sensitive and lack confidence especially suffer. According to Education.com, "Children who are bullied are at greater risk of depression and lower self-esteem later in life, prone to missing more school, and more likely to have problems with alcohol and drug use." As the media has shown, bullying can even lead to suicide.

Bullying Can Go Unnoticed

Unlike fighting, which is more easily observed, bullying is frequently less visible to the adults in charge or is seen as a non-issue. However, it does erode discipline and student and staff morale. Furthermore, prolonged bullying can cause explosive violence. When youths are intimidated and, believing no one cares, the bullied person may retaliate with rage to oneself or to bullies.

Bullying often occurs in PE, recess, hallways, bathrooms, and school buses, while waiting for buses or in classes requiring group work or after school activities. Students can bully others as individuals or as a group. Some forms of bullying can come from cliques. When I taught high school, some students insisted there were no such exclusive groups in their class. But others who felt left out grumbled their disagreement. Bullying can be blind.

Working Together

Bullying hurts the teaching mission of the school. Grades often drop because worry transforms energy that should be spent on studies into fear that no one will sit with them at lunch or other bullying-related tactics.

Today's schools have policies regarding bullying. The policies need to be implemented by dedicated teachers and administration. Bullying decreases and stops when teachers, parents, administrators, and other significant adults refuse to tolerate it or other violence. Home and school must cooperate to eliminate bullying and teach students to respect each other.

Students make a good school better when they respect and affirm teachers and classmates. In 1 Thessalonians 5:11 it says, "Therefore encourage one another and build one another up, as indeed you do."

Our youth deserve respect and the chance to learn. Bullying can weaken their opportunities for learning and hurt the common good. Let us pray that with adult example, guidance, and supervision, bullies see and repent of damages they cause, change, and mature. This would make bullied youth, their concerned families, teachers, and others who support our schools, happy.

IV: LENT

Article 1: Making a Fruitful Lenten Confession

A Catholic convert in her 60's made her first Lenten confession. As she confessed her sins, she began to weep. The priest listened and gently asked only a few questions. She exclaimed, "He was so understanding and non-judgmental. It was easy for me to open up and confess."

She remembers sobbing tears of gratitude for the healing feeling and weight gone from her shoulders. After receiving absolution, she said that she felt drained, but very uplifted.

Since that first face-to-face Confession, she has always chosen the anonymity of the confessional. But two things remain the same: she always cries and always comes away feeling healed. This priest was not the master of forgiveness but God's servant of forgiveness.

Philip Kosoloski wrote an article entitled, "The Key to Making a Good Confession That Will Change Your Life Forever." The article is based upon the Catechetical Instructions of St. John Vianney, the patron saint of all priests, who heard Confessions sometimes 16 hours a day and made the unlikely village of Ars the European capitol of Confession.

He believed that if we realized how much our sins helped to put Jesus on the cross, we might weep as the woman convert and St. Peter did.

St. Peter, who bragged that he would never deny Christ, denied him three times on Good Friday. After Peter's third denial as soldiers led Jesus past Peter, Jesus looked with forgiveness into Peter's eyes, the windows of his soul. Peter wept because he recognized that though his sins helped to crucify Christ, Christ forgave him.

In John 20:19-23 on Easter evening, Jesus breathed on the apostles and said, "Receive the Holy Spirit, whose sins you forgive are forgiven them, and whose sins you retain are retained."

Cross is Reminder of Christ's Death

The late Fr. Joseph De Stefano said, as Anton Grauel, a famous artist, carved a huge crucifix for a Beloit church, a friend found him in tears as he contemplated the crucified Christ.

The Venerable Fulton Sheen said that the crucifix reminds us that when Jesus died on the cross, he "offered his life to the Father to make reparation for our sinful disobedience." His saving life, death, and resurrection repaired humanity's relationship with God, lost by the sin of Adam and Eve."

Sacrament Process

Important steps of receiving the Sacrament of Reconciliation fruitfully include facing up to our sins in a culture which often tends to deny sin, being sorry for them, confessing them, and making an "Act of Contrition."

In perfect contrition, we are sorry for our sins because we have offended God who is all good and deserving of all our love.

In imperfect contrition we are sorry for our sins because we dread the loss of heaven and pains of hell.

Next, the priest gives us a penance. In No.1459 of the Catechism of the Catholic Church, it says, "Many sins wrong our neighbor. One must do what is possible in order to repair the harm (e.g., return stolen goods, help to restore the reputation of someone slandered, pay compensation for injuries, and the like). Sin also injures and weakens the sinner himself and his relationships with God and neighbor.

In No. 1460 of the Catechism of the Catholic Church, it says "The penance the confessor imposes can consist of prayer, an offering, works of mercy, service of neighbor, voluntary self-denial, sacrifices, and above all, the patient acceptance of the cross we must bear. Such penances help configure us to Christ, who alone expiated our sins once and for all."

We also promise to amend our life and avoid occasions of sin which takes God's help. The steps of confession, the "Act of Contrition," and absolution make good meditations.

The Sacrament of Penance reconciles us with the Church but has also a revitalizing effect on the Church which suffers from her members' sins. Since Reconciliation is the sacrament of conversion, Pope Francis urges us to join him and receive the Sacrament of Reconciliation during Lent, the season of conversion.

Article 2: Lent Calls Us to a Deeper Conversion

In the Peanuts comic strip, each fall Lucy held the football for Charlie Brown to kick. At the last second, Lucy picked up the ball and Charlie Brown missed it and fell flat on his face.

After years of being tricked, Charlie refused to kick the football because he no longer trusted Lucy. She broke down, shed tears, and confessed, "I have sinned. I want to change. Won't you give me another chance, please!" Charlie Brown trusted her again.

But again, Lucy pulled the ball and Charlie fell flat on his face. Lucy defended herself by saying, "Recognizing your faults and truly changing are two different things, Charlie Brown."

Striving to Change

The 40 days of Lent invites us who are baptized and those preparing to be baptized or converts who are received into the Church to recognize our sins and faults. Then through grace, we are to strive to change into more Christ-like persons.

Lent prepares us to renew our Baptismal promises at Easter when we celebrate the resurrection, the heart of our faith. Lent is the season of final preparation for those who will be baptized and/or received into the Church at the Easter Vigil. The Church invites us who are already baptized to pray for them.

Ash Wednesday

On Ash Wednesday we indicate our desire to change by receiving the cross of ashes. The ashes indicate our willingness to take up our cross and do penance for Lent.

The priest or deacon says, "Remember, you are dust and unto dust, you shall return." These words remind us of the mortality of our body and the immortality of our soul. The body upon which we lavish so much attention will turn to dust. The soul which we may ignore will live forever.

The alternate words which accompany the distribution of ashes are "Repent and believe the Good News." The ashes remind us that we will die. But there is still time to repent and believe the Good News, Lent invites us to seriously ask, "How can we live our baptismal promises better? How are we doing in our quest for heaven?"

Penance and Prayer

Since the early centuries, the Church has urged Catholics to choose a Lenten penance. In my opinion, Lent is the season when Catholics respond best to parish programs, devotions, and penance. The Ash Wednesday Gospel recommends that we choose a penance based upon prayer, fasting, or almsgiving.

Prayer deepens our relationship with God and helps us to discern and do God's will as did Mary. We might ask, "How do we pray? Should we pray more? As a family or individually, we can pray the Rosary, participate in Mass, attend devotions, do spiritual reading, or other forms of prayer."

Prayer opens us to the grace of almsgiving. It enables us to see and respond to the needy. In Matthew 26:40, Jesus says, "Amen, I say to you, whatever you did for one of these least brothers of mine, you did for me." We minister to the needy by contributing to food pantries, helping hidden poor in our midst, sponsoring a third world child, or by visiting and affirming the self-worth of shut ins.

Fasting and Call to Holiness

The Ash Wednesday Gospel also recommends fasting. In nos. 2013 and 2015 of the Catechism of the Catholic Church it says that all Christians in any state of life are called to holiness, Spiritual perfection passes by way of the cross. To live the Gospel, we must daily struggle to die to self and sin and rise to new life in Jesus. In Colossians 3:1-2, it says, "If then you were raised with Christ, seek what is above, where Christ is seated at the right hand of God. Think of what is above, not is of earth."

The Lenten rules for fasting and abstaining are that every person 14 years of age or older must abstain from meat (and items made with meat) on Ash Wednesday, Good Friday, and all Fridays of Lent. Every person between ages 18 and 60 must fast on Ash Wednesday and Good Friday.

In Isaiah 58:7, it says that fasting should result in "sharing your bread with the hungry, sheltering the oppressed and the homeless, clothing the naked when you see them," and the like. During Lent we are encouraged to receive the Sacrament of Reconciliation which strengthens us to fast from sins such as grudges, resentments, and revenge.

Our response to Lent's graces can help us to recognize our sins and faults and change day by day into more Christ-like persons. May our Lenten participation help us to renew our baptismal promises at Easter, grow into a more Christ-like person in this world, and enjoy the fullness of Eternal Life.

Receiving the Eucharist worthily strengthens us to live the Gospel on earth. In John 6:54 it says, "Whoever eats my flesh and drinks my blood has eternal life, and I will raise him on the last day." May we truly become more like Jesus during Lent.

3: Lent Has Surprisingly Modern Appeal

Christians around the world mark Lent's beginning by celebrating Ash Wednesday. Lent has a surprising modern appeal. Some pastors say that next to Christmas, people come to church on Ash Wednesday more than on any other day.

Facing a Basic Truth

Receiving ashes helps us face a basic truth that we may try to avoid, namely, that we will die. The priest or deacon says, "Remember, you are dust and to dust you shall return." They may also say, "Repent and believe the Good News." Combined, the words remind us that we will die and return to dust; therefore, while we're still alive, we are to repent and believe the Good News! During Lent we are to choose a penance that helps us become a more Christ-like person. Often our penance is a form of prayer, fasting, and/or almsgiving that Ash Wednesday's Gospel recommends.

Improving Our Prayer Life

As a Lenten penance, we can examine and improve our prayer life. Do we pray mechanically, or do we raise our minds and hearts to God? Do we pray emergencies or is prayer a daily practice?

Do we study the Mass so we can participate fully, actively, and pray the Rosary, morning and evening prayers, and/or Divine Mercy devotions?

Fasting and Abstinence

During Lent, the Church requires most Catholics to fast. Everyone between the age of 18 and 59 must fast on Ash Wednesday and Good

Friday. (Fasting means only one full meal a day.). Everyone 14 years of age or older must abstain from meat on Ash Wednesday, Good Friday, and all Fridays of Lent.

Medieval monks fasted from butter, lard, and fat. They celebrated an Ash Wednesday ceremony called "Burying the Fat" in which they put butter in a casket and actually buried it. They took it seriously because they believed it was their way to sharing in Christ's suffering.

Giving up some food items may be healthy and sacrificial, but during Lent we can also bury the hatchet and forgive those who hurt us. We can bury our selfishness and give more of our time, talent, and treasure to serve others. We can bury our indifference and rise earlier to spend time in prayer, attend Mass, or do spiritual reading.

Giving to Others

Another penance is almsgiving, giving money or food to poor people. Lent asks us to repent of selfishness that ignores the needs of the poor and rationalizes that we can satisfy our obligations toward them by gifts of surplus wealth without examining unjust structures that cause poverty.

Family Practices

As their children's primary religious educators, parents should encourage their children to choose a Lenten penance. The family can also do penances together, sponsoring a Third World child, or visiting a shut-in or senior citizen. Parents can make Fridays of Lent a special reminder of Christ's sacrifice. Praising God as a family helps bring families closer together. Patrick Peyton, the "Rosary priest," stated, "The family that prays together, stays together."

Pope Francis has recommended ten areas that can help us choose a Lenten penance: 1) Get rid of the lazy addiction to evil that deceives us and ensnares us; 2) Do something that hurts; 3) Don't remain indifferent; 4) Pray: Make our hearts like Yours; 5) Take part in the sacraments; 6) More intense prayer; 7) Almsgiving; 8) Fasting; 9) Help the poor; and 10) Evangelize!

In these and other ways, Lent prepares us to renew our baptismal promises at Easter with deepened faith. During the Easter Triduum, we remember that Christ died for our sins and rose from the dead so that we could enjoy Heaven's eternal joy.

May we enjoy a fruitful Lent that helps us live the Easter season and be renewed in faith and Easter joy!

4: Lent Calls Us to Grow in our Easter Faith

When Matt Hasselbeck, the Seattle Seahawks quarterback, was a Boston College junior, he volunteered to spend eight days in the missions of Jamaica during spring break. The people's poverty shocked him. But their faith, especially the faith of George McVee, a leper, inspired him.

George, a horribly disfigured leper, had no money, no nose, no feet or hands. Yet he daily thanked God for his blessings.

Inspired by George's faith, Matt promised God that despite setbacks, he would always do his best. George's good example helped Matt to appreciate his blessings and to grow as a Catholic and football player.

Invitation to Grow in Faith

During Lent, we seek to grow in our faith as Matt did. Lent's 40 days remind us of the 40 days that Jesus spent in the desert preparing for his public ministry after his Baptism.

Lent invites both baptized Catholics and Rite of Christian Initiation of Adults (RCIA) catechumens and candidates preparing to become Catholics, to grow in their faith. A candidate can have been legitimately baptized in another Christian faith.

After a long preparation, the candidate makes a profession of faith and receives the Sacraments of Confirmation and Eucharist at the Easter Vigil or when he or she is ready. At the Easter Vigil, catechumens are baptized, confirmed, and receive the Eucharist. During the Easter Vigil, the baptized are invited to renew their Baptism promises.

A Sign of Our Commitment

We begin Lent on Ash Wednesday when we receive a cross of ashes. The ashes remind us that our body upon which we lavish so much attention will turn to dust. The soul that we sometimes neglect will live forever.

Receiving the ashes is a sign of our commitment to choose a Lenten penance that helps us to grow in Jesus' image. The words accompanying the imposition of ashes are "Remember, man you are dust and unto dust you shall return."

The alternate words are "Turn away from sin and be faithful to the Gospel." One combined message of both is that while we yet are alive, we are to repent and believe and live the Good News.

Called to be "Perfect"

In No. 2013 of the Catechism of the Catholic Church, it says, "All Christians in any state or walk of life are called to fullness of Christian life and to the perfection of charity. All are called to holiness: 'Be perfect as your heavenly Father is perfect.'"

In No. 2015 of the Catechism of the Catholic Church it says, the way of perfection passes by way of the Cross. There is no holiness without renunciation and spiritual battle. Spiritual progress entails the ascesis (self-discipline) and mortification that gradually leads to living in the peace and joy of the Beatitudes.

For centuries the Church has asked Catholics to choose a penance of prayer, fasting, or almsgiving for Lent.

Prayer can deepen our relationship with God and help us to participate fully, consciously, and actively in the Mass. During Lent we can go to daily Mass if we can, pray the Rosary, participate in devotions, or pray for others.

Fasting: Not Just from Food

Catholics between ages 18 and 59 are obliged to fast on Ash Wednesday and Good Friday. In addition, all Catholics 14 years of age and older must abstain from meat on Ash Wednesday, Good Friday, and all the Fridays of Lent.

Fasting and abstaining make us realize how trapped we are in the culture of self-gratification. Those who fast experience a personal liberation.

Fasting means more than fasting from food. In Isaiah 58:6-7 it says, "This is the fasting that I wish: releasing those bound unjustly, untying the thongs of the yoke; setting free the oppressed, breaking every yoke; sharing your bread with the hungry, sheltering the oppressed and the homeless; clothing the naked when you see them, and not turning your back on your own."

We can fast from gossip, criticism, grudges, resentments, revenge, and the like. We can fast from being in control and having a need to dominate and control others. Fasting from food should be accompanied by a loving and forgiving attitude toward others.

Another Lenten penance can be almsgiving. Ideally the alms or time that we share should somehow bring us into solidarity with the people we help. We can contribute to help Haiti and other countries recover from tragedies. We can volunteer at homeless shelters or help the hidden poor in our midst. We can sponsor and write to a third World child, contribute to food pantries, or visit shut ins.

Spiritual Growth

Prayer opens us to grace and strengthens us to see and respond to the needy. Helping the poor is a response to Jesus' words, "Amen, I say to you, whatever you did for one of these least brothers of mine, you did for me."

The word Lent comes from a Teutonic word which means springtime. May our Lent be a springtime of spiritual growth as spring break was for Matt Hasselbeck and other volunteers."

May we enjoy a graced Lent that helps us grow in Easter faith.

5: Fr. Mazzuchelli's Example

We begin Lent on March 1 by receiving a cross of ashes on our forehead. The ashes remind us that we are dust and unto dust we shall return.

Receiving the ashes also reminds us that while we are still alive, we are to repent and believe the Good News so that at Easter we can renew our Baptismal promises with deepened faith.

Venerable Fr. Samuel Mazzuchelli died on February 23, 1864, during Lent. Thanks especially to the Sinsinawa Dominican Sisters, we know much about Father Samuel, who reflects many of Pope Francis' virtues. Both can inspire us to live Lent in a Christ-like way that helps us continue our journey to heaven.

Brought church to Tri-State Area

Father Mazzuchelli was an immigrant Italian Dominican friar and missionary who heroically helped bring the Church to the Iowa-Wisconsin-Illinois tri-state area and to upper Wisconsin-Michigan. He died as pastor of St. Patrick Church, Benton; founded the Sinsinawa

Dominican Sisters; and accomplished so much more that I get tired just thinking about how much he did.

After he died, an iron penance chain embedded in his flesh was discovered which he secretly wore in order to be more fully united with Christ's suffering. His fasting and many hardships weren't enough to express his love for his all-loving redeemer. He wanted to do more.

At Sinsinawa Mound the penance chain is available for veneration. Those who reflect upon it find it a powerful reminder of his sacrifices and selfless service. Upon request, interested visitors, along with a Sister, can pray in the presence of the chain.

Devotion to Our Lady of Sorrows

Father Mazzuchelli had a deep devotion to Our Lady of Sorrows whose image hung above his bed. After he died, Fr. John Kinsella, his confessor, revealed that Father Samuel told him that he had a vision of Mary. He exclaimed that he had never seen anyone as beautiful as Christ's mother!

Father Mazzuchelli died as he lived, ministering to others. Like Pope Francis, he had a deep respect for the elderly.

On February 15, 1864, an old woman requested the last sacraments. As he hurried to her sickbed, he experienced chills and severe pains. A physician diagnosed that he had pleura pneumonia. Loyal Dominican Sisters kept an unbroken vigil of prayer on his behalf. Fourteen of these Sisters are buried next to him at Benton.

A Priest of the Poor

Like Pope Francis, whom some call the pope of the poor, he was the priest of the poor. A parishioner wrote, "In Father Samuel we recognized the pious energetic priest, the true friend who constantly served the poor and suffering."

In 1850 when a cholera epidemic struck New Diggings, Senator James Earnest helped Father Samuel care for the sick. Susan, his daughter wrote, "I have heard my father tell of the New Diggings' cholera epidemic. Nearly every family was afflicted. Father Samuel and my father worked shoulder to shoulder, giving the sick help and comfort."

Father Samuel adopted four orphan boys. He placed little girls in other families. When a mother died in childbirth, he asked the Dominican Sisters to care for her two-year-old daughter and her newborn infant. They did for two years.

He also transacted wills and bequests hastily made by dying Protestants, Catholics, and others. Like Pope Francis, he championed the rights of the oppressed, defended poor settlers' rights, and Catholic soldiers' right to attend Sunday Mass at Fort Mackinac.

He opposed the Indian Removal Act. He defended the Indians' right to land, natural resources, and their children's education. On their behalf, he sent protests to Indian agents, the governor of Michigan territory, the Wisconsin delegate to Congress, and even to the United States president.

Became American Citizen

Father Mazzuchelli, who became an American citizen, admired America, but he was not afraid to criticize its shortcomings.

President Lincoln asked that America have a National Day of Thanksgiving on August 6, 1863 for recent union victories. Father Samuel, who vehemently opposed slavery, was invited to preach on that day in Galena.

To everyone's surprise, he assumed a prophet's unpopular stance. He asked, "How can we lift up our voices in united prayers of thanksgiving while our beloved country is distracted, humbled, and brought low by the most destructive warfare history has ever recorded."

Like Pope Francis he worked tirelessly for peace. In a 2015 talk, Pope Francis suggested that instead of giving up chocolate or alcohol for Lent, we give up indifference. He added that, "When we become indifferent, we may become incapable of feeling compassion at the poor's outcry and feel no need to help them as though this were someone else's responsibility and not ours."

Lent is a graced time to learn more about Pope Francis, Father Mazzuchelli, and other saintly persons. They can inspire us to follow Christ as they did. Let's also continue to pray that the Church honors Venerable Fr. Samuel Mazzuchelli with the title of Blessed soon.

6: A Time for Fasting and Praying

Lent is a time for fasting. When we think of fasting, we probably think of fasting and abstaining from food and drink for the sake of Jesus according to the Lenten regulations. However, in Isaiah 58:1-9, through Isaiah, God reveals another kind of fasting that enables us to feast and feed on living God's way more fully. God wants fasting that releases those bound unjustly, sets free the oppressed, breaks every yoke, shares bread with the hungry, shelters the oppressed and the homeless, clothes the naked, does not turn away from our own, and similar works of compassionate love and mercy.

Suggestions for Fasting/Feasting

Here are a few suggestions for this kind of fasting and feasting. The Holy Spirit will surely show us more ways if we ask:

- Fast from fear. Feast on faith.
- Abstain from despair, Feed on hope.
- Fast from rudeness. Feast on politeness.
- Abstain from stinginess. Feed those in need from our pantries of want and abundance.
- Fast from spreading bad news. Feast on spreading God's Good News.
- Abstain from taking our blessings for granted. Feed on gratitude for our blessings.
- Fast from violence. Feast on sharing God's gift of peace.
- Abstain from impatience. Feed on patience.
- Fast from poor sportsmanship. Feast on good sportsmanship.
- Abstain from gossip. Feed on praising the goodness of others.
- Fast from cursing and swearing. Feast on reverencing God's Holy Name.
- Abstain from disrespect. Feed on respect for others and all God's creation.

- Fast from insensitivity to the pain of others. Feast on Christ-like compassion.
- Abstain from dishonesty and insincerity. Feed on honesty and sincerity.
- Fast from blind and deaf criticism. Feast on announcing the goodness in the character of others.
- Abstain from resentment. Feed on love and forgiveness.
- Fast from words that wound. Feast on words that heal.
- Abstain from excessive, mindless chatter. Feed on listening in graced silence.
- Fast from gloom. Feast on healthy Catholic joy and humor.
- Abstain from "Martha" busyness. Pray that Jesus feeds us with "Mary's better part."

Through Isaiah, God promises that if we fast in these ways, then we shall call upon the Lord and the Lord will answer. We shall cry for help and God will say, "Here I am!"

Making Good Choices

We may have already chosen our Lenten penance. But even if we have, these suggestions can remind us that Lent is a season of grace that invites us to make and affirm good choices.

The choices we make can help to make us grow more fully in God's image. Living a good Lent can also prepare us to celebrate Easter and Pentecost with renewed faith.

Good choices affect us in time and Eternity. The time to make and/or affirm our choice of a Lenten penance that helps us grow in the image of Jesus is NOW!

V: SPRING

Chapter One: St. Joseph

1: Instrument of God's Mercy

A friend sent me a Christmas card that he proudly created. It featured a picture of Mary lovingly holding the infant Jesus. Under the picture were the words, "Who is Missing?"

The answer is St. Joseph, who as the head of the Holy Family, was there to support Mary as she gave birth to Jesus on Christmas. We honor him as a great saint because he was the foster father of Jesus who with Mary guided young Jesus as he grew in wisdom, understanding, and knowledge.

Role as Protector

Joseph exercised his role as protector of Mary and Jesus discreetly, humbly, and silently. He did so with an unfailing presence and fidelity, even when he found it difficult and confusing.

From the time of his betrothal to Mary until the finding of the 12-year old Jesus in the Jerusalem Temple, he was there at every moment with loving care. As Mary's spouse, he was at her side in good times and bad on the journey to Bethlehem for the census and in the anxious and joyful hours when she gave birth.

He led and protected the Holy Family during the flight into Egypt, during the frantic search for their child in the Temple, and later in the day-to-day life in his Nazareth home. At his workshop, St. Joseph taught his carpenter trade to Jesus.

Stayed in The Background

When we contemplate the saints in heaven, we may be dazzled by their colors, talents, and the depth of their accomplishments. But, when we come to St. Joseph, we might wonder what dazzling colors do we find in him?

Not the red of the martyrs, nor the gold of a world leader, nor the pulpit of a great preacher, nor the scroll of a great author. Sometimes he is called Joseph the Silent, because he never spoke a word in Scripture. He very rightfully stayed in the background to Jesus and Mary.

His uniqueness is that no other saint besides the Blessed Mother could say that every day for almost 30 years he sat at table with the young boy who was the Son of God. Daily he watched him grow into manhood. He taught him his prayers. He showed him how to make chairs and tables. Who could count the times he held Jesus in his arms when he was little, or the times Jesus hugged him and kissed him? Who could count the meals they ate together, the miles they traveled together, or the joy they had in working together?

Honoring St. Joseph

In front of Beloit Catholic High was a statue of St. Joseph, the Worker, with the teenage Jesus. There was also a statue of St. Joseph, the Worker, at Beloit's St. Paul Catholic Church. These statues remind us that as Mary's husband and Jesus' foster father, he worked as a carpenter to help provide for the Holy Family. He also supported and protected them through his active, courageous love.

A surprising number of parishes are named in honor of St. Joseph. They remind us to continue to admire and respect St. Joseph, the husband of Mary and patron saint of fathers. He spoke not only with words but especially with his deeds.

He was truly an instrument of God's mercy as he lived the Corporal and Spiritual Works of Mercy. Let us imitate his loyalty and faithfulness to Jesus and his devotion to Mary and ask for his intercession.

2: St. Joseph, the Worker, Inspires and Helps Workers

On May 1st, we Catholics celebrate the Feast of St Joseph, the Worker. St. Joseph is the patron saint of workers.

Throughout our diocese, statues of St. Joseph the Worker show him holding a saw, eager to give another day's work to help support Jesus and Mary. His example reminds us of the graced work, sweat, and sacrifice that go into the building of our churches both physically and spiritually. He reminds us that honest work can be a grace or ladder to God.

In paragraph 2460 of the Catechism of the Catholic Church, it is stated, "By means of labor, humanity participates in the work of creation. Work united to Christ can be redemptive."

As we know, there are times when jobs are scarce and unemployment increases. Such a time is now!

In paragraph 2436 of the Catechism of the Catholic Church it is stated, "Unemployment almost always wounds its victim's dignity and threatens the equilibrium of his life. Besides the harm done to him personally, it entails many risks for his family."

Supporting the Unemployed

In the March-April issue of Discipleship Journal, Stacey Shannon shares some little ways that we can encourage and support the unemployed for a year.

First, she suggests that it is good to periodically ask how the unemployed are doing and make time to listen. However, she warned against offering advice unless they ask for it.

Second, Stacey Shannon suggests that we can help by planning budget friendly activities. We can invite unemployed friends over for a meal or treat them to a dinner out. We can rent a DVD rather than catching a fully paid movie or hitting the mall.

Third, she suggests that we should be tactful about how we go about offering financial help. Perhaps we can contribute anonymously with cash or giving a gift certificate to a grocery store or restaurant.

Finally, Stacy Shannon says that we can share our prayers. She knew that others prayed for them, but hearing that they did by phone, email, and during visits provided extra encouragement.

The Power of Prayer

Alfred Lord Tennyson wrote that "more things are wrought by prayer than this world dreams of." In How to Stop Worrying and Start Living by Dale Carnegie, the faith and prayers of his mother held their family together during years of hard times. They saved her husband's life.

Others say that if the unemployed has a spouse, we should not neglect him or her. We can give them the opportunity to express how they feel. We might also encourage them to occasionally play, have fun, and try to stay positive.

Despite its hardship, sometimes unemployment can cause us to simplify our lives, discover new talents, deepen our faith, and help us to appreciate what we have and don't have. To do this, we need God's grace.

Intercession of St. Joseph

We can also ask the intercession of St. Joseph for the unemployed because he experienced it. When Herod tried to kill Jesus, Joseph had to leave his thriving carpenter business in Nazareth and flee to Egypt with a minimum of possessions. There he had to begin again to find work and new customers. When he returned to Nazareth, he had to start over again. But he did not do this alone. Mary, his faithful wife, shared his crosses and prayed for and supported her husband.

St. Joseph's example can help to bring meaning to our work. We can also ask his intercession and guidance for the unemployed. We can pray that God gifts them with patience, perseverance, and positive hope.

May we enjoy a blessed Feast of St. Joseph, the Worker. Have a blessed Easter Season!

Chapter Two: Easter

1: Easter Faith Reveals Flowers of Hope

A boy returned from catechism class, where he learned about Jesus Resurrection. He was excited. During his walk home, he stopped at a religious goods store to study a crucifix in the window.

An elderly man joined him. He seemed confused by the crucifix.

Sharing His Faith

Eager to share his faith, the boy exclaimed, "Sir, please don't be confused. I can explain everything. That's Jesus on the cross. He died for our sins. The beautiful lady under the cross is Mary, his mother. She's crying because some bad guys crucified her son."

Tears blinded the man as he hobbled painfully away. The boy's faith reminded him of the faith he once had.

The boy shouted after him, "Sir, please don't cry. I forgot the best part. Some bad guys crucified Jesus; but his Father raised him from the dead. Now he is in heaven as good as new. He wants to take us there to be with him after we die. I can't wait!"

Heart of Christianity

This boy's faith points to Jesus' Resurrection, which is at the heart of Christianity. In 1 Corinthians 15:14, St. Paul teaches, "If Christ has not been raised from the dead, then our preaching is in vain and our faith empty."

On Good Friday, the apostles' faith was weakened when Jesus was crucified. Peter denied that he even knew Jesus. Fearing they would be next, the apostles hid.

After Jesus rose and appeared to the apostles and other followers, their hopes were resurrected, too. At Pentecost, they were changed into courageous witnesses for Jesus. All except John died for Jesus. The Church spread rapidly from Jerusalem to Samaria to the ends of the earth.

Flower Offers Hope

Greta Weissman, a Nazi concentration camp survivor, recalls how she and other inmates stood for an hour, waiting to barely survive on some poor prison food that tasted like slop. They nearly collapsed from hunger, fatigue, and lack of hope.

Then, she noticed that in a corner of this horrid, hopeless place, the concrete had been broken, leaving a crack. A flower had pushed through the tiny crack. For those who had very little for which to hope, the tiny flower offered hope and beauty.

Every morning thousands of feet on the way to forced labor or roll call shuffled to avoid stepping on their precious symbol of beauty and hope which nourished their will to live. The flower reminds us that Jesus rose from the tomb of stone and gives meaning and hope to believers.

Hope in Eternal Life

We Catholics believe that life is not a dead-end street with no exit, as Jean Paul Sartre taught; rather, when we live our baptismal promises, death opens the door to eternal life. Belief in the resurrection gives us hope. Thanks to Jesus, we believe that though life has its wonderful moments, these are nothing compared to eternal life,

In number 1003 of the *Catechism of the Catholic Church* it says, "United with Christ by Baptism, believers already truly participate in the heavenly life of the risen Christ, but this life remains hidden with Christ in God.

"The Father has already raised us up with him and made us sit with him in the heavenly places in Christ Jesus. Nourished with his body in the Eucharist, we already belong to the body of Christ. When we rise on the last day, *we* will also appear with him in glory."

Flowers of Hope

Like the tiny concentration camp flower, Easter lilies are flowers of hope because they remind us of resurrection, the heart of our faith.

Belief in the resurrection gives us hope. Sometimes our lamp of hope dims low—a broken relationship, unexpected illness, lack of faith, loss of a friend, unemployment, or other unexpected blows weaken our hope. Then, a flower of hope in the form of encouragement, prayer, or support in unexpected ways strengthens our hope.

A friend told me that he hopes to enjoy a risen glorified body in heaven. This has deeper meaning, because he is disabled, had a leg amputated, and severe spinal problems; yet, he rarely complains. He truly is God's flower of hope to me and others.

Easter signifies a rebirth and a new beginning for believers in this life and beyond into eternity. In First Corinthians 2:9 it says, "Eye has not seen, nor ear heard, nor it entered the human heart what God has prepared for those who love him."

Each day God sends flowers of hope into our life. Let us pray for the Easter faith to see these flowers with Jesus' eyes. Each day let us ask the Holy Spirit to empower us to live and share our Easter faith as Jesus desires.

Let us renew and live our baptismal promises with deepened faith that reflects our hope of eternal life and helps us be flowers of hope to those in need. May we be eternally thankful for Jesus' Resurrection during and beyond the Easter season. Alleluia! Christ has risen! Let us be glad and rejoice!

2: Easter's Eternal Surprise

In February 1991, during Operation Desert Storm, Ruth Dillow received the sad news from the Pentagon that her son Clayton had stepped on a mine in Kuwait and was killed.

Ruth said that the grief and shock she felt was almost unbearable. For three days she wept constantly. For three days family and friends tried to comfort her, but they could not. Her grief was too great! She felt some of the grief that Mary surely experienced when her son, Jesus, was crucified.

Surprising News

After the third day, the telephone rang. "It's just another stranger trying to comfort me," she thought. Reluctantly, she picked up the phone. The voice on the phone shouted joyfully, "Mom, it's me. I'm still alive! It's me!"

Ruth exclaimed, "I couldn't believe it at first. But gradually I recognized Clayton's voice. The earlier news of his death was a mistake." She laughed. She cried. She felt like doing cartwheels because Clayton was alive.

When Christ was crucified on Good Friday, the apostles' hopes and dreams were crucified with him.

The shock of Jesus' crucifixion was so great that Peter, the leader of the apostles, denied that he knew Christ. He and the apostles ran away and hid because they feared they might be crucified next; but then came the surprise of Easter.

In John 20: 1-2 Mary Magdalene went to the tomb on Easter morning. It was still dark, which reflected a "Good Friday world" without resurrection and hope. Mary Magdalene was the first to discover that the stone had been rolled away and the tomb was empty. She was also the first to tell others about the empty tomb.

Later the burial wrappings on the ground and the piece of cloth that had covered his head, not lying with the wrappings but rolled up in a separate place, were discovered. Another surprise was the appearance of the Risen Lord to the apostles and other followers. According to First Corinthians 15:6, Jesus appeared to more than 500 followers at one time.

Apostles' Transformation

Spiritual writers believe that another convincing sign of Jesus' resurrection is the apostles' transformation. After they experienced the Risen Lord and received the Holy Spirit, they were changed from frightened and confused followers, who on Good Friday denied Jesus and hid, into his courageous witnesses. Every Apostle except John, who cared for Mary, died for the faith.

In the almost 2,000 years since then, the Holy Spirit has transformed many others and helped them live and die for the faith. In Romans 8:11 it says, "If the spirit of the one who raised Jesus from the dead dwells in you, the one who raised Christ from the dead will give life to your mortal bodies also, through his Spirit that dwells in you."

In No. 1002 of the Catechism of the Catholic Church it says, "Christ will raise us up on the last day, but it is also true, that in a certain way, we have already risen with Christ. For by virtue of the Holy Spirit, Christian life is already a participation in the death and resurrection of Christ."

Hope Flows from Our Faith

Pope Benedict XVI once said that the crisis of faith is really a crisis of spiritual hope. Most of us have certain earthly hopes such as financial security, health, a happy vocation, a better world for our children; but we also need to embrace the ultimate hope that gives meaning and purpose to everything we do.

This hope flows from our faith in the Risen Jesus who promises us the gift of heaven when we live our Baptism promises, which we renew at Easter!

A father revealed that the loss of his young son in a tragic accident gave Easter new meaning. He explained, "Before the accident, I always thought that Easter was a nice day with bunny rabbits and Easter eggs, but when someone precious like my son died, Easter became everything: an anchor in a fierce storm, a rock on which to stand, a hope that raised me above despair and kept me going."

During a Catholic funeral Mass, we express our hope that the person whose funeral we celebrate will rise with a new glorified body. Because of the resurrection, we believe that for believers, life is not a dead end with no exit, but the door to eternal life.

Theologian Wolfhart Pannenberg said, "The evidence for Jesus' resurrection is so strong that nobody would question it except for two things: First, it is a very unusual event. Second, if you believe it happened, you have to change the way you live!" This takes graced daily effort, but the benefits are Heavenly!

In First Corinthians 2:9 it says, "Eye has not seen, and ear has not heard, nor has it so much as dawned on man what God has prepared for those who love him."

This passage reveals that Heaven will be Easter's Eternal surprise because seeing God face to face will fill us with a joy that is beyond our present finite comprehension.

3: May Our Lives Sing the Song that Jesus Lives

A great conductor rehearsed a choir for a performance of the Messiah. The chorus sang through to the part where the soprano sings, "I Know That My Redeemer Lives."

Her singing was flawless: perfect phrasing, pitch, enunciation, and all of the singing qualities that I wish I had. When she finished, the choir waited eagerly for the applause that would surely follow.

Instead, the conductor glared at the soloist and growled, "My dear, you do not really believe that your Redeemer lives, do you?"

Shaken, the girl replied, "Why yes, I think so!"

"Then sing it," begged the conductor. "Sing it in such a way that everyone feels the power and joy of your belief."

The conductor wanted the soprano's singing to reflect her faith that "Jesus lives" because he has risen.

Hopes, Dreams of Jesus' Followers

The resurrection of Jesus was the central theme of apostolic preaching. In 1 Corinthians 15:13-14, St. Paul proclaims, "If there is no resurrection of the dead, then neither has Christ been raised, and if Christ has not been raised, then empty (too) is our preaching; empty, too, your faith."

When the sun sank into the earth on Good Friday, the hopes and dreams of most of Jesus' followers were buried with him. They hoped that he was the messiah who would establish a mighty earthly kingdom. Instead he allowed himself to be crucified like a criminal. His apostles lost hope and hid.

When the apostles heard the good news that Jesus rose from the dead on Easter morning, their hopes and dreams rose with him. In the *Catechism of the Catholic Church*, it says, "The empty tomb and the linen cloths lying there signify in themselves that by God's power, Christ's body had escaped the bonds of death and corruption. They prepared the disciples to encounter the Risen Lord."

When they encountered the Risen Lord and received the Holy Spirit, the apostles and other followers who deserted Christ were transformed into courageous witnesses of Christ. They helped to spread the gospel "to the ends of the earth." Eleven of the 12 apostles died for Christ.

Participation in the Resurrection

The good news of Easter is that because Christ has risen, resurrection can happen in our lives now and for eternity. In the *Catechism of the Catholic Church*, it says, "Christ will raise us up 'on the last day'; but it is also true that, in a certain way, we have already risen with Christ. For, by virtue of the Holy Spirit, Christian life is already now on earth a participation in the death and resurrection of Christ."

Our incorporation into the death and resurrection of Christ is brought about through Baptism, the Easter sacrament. During the Easter vigil, catechumens are baptized and all of us are called to renew our baptismal promises.

We reveal that our Redeemer lives in us by doing what is right and by being instruments of God's love in our families, work, church, and recreation. Easter offers us the hope we need to wipe away our tears, pick up the pieces, and start again after tragedy. As baptized Catholics, we believe in the sun of hope even when it is not shining because we know it will shine again.

Encountering Christ in the Eucharist

The Eucharist is another Easter sacrament. In John 6:54, Jesus promised, "Whoever eats my flesh and drinks my blood has eternal life, and I will raise him on the last day," In *On the Merits and Forgiveness of Sins and on Infant Baptism*, St. Augustine taught that by truly encountering Christ in the Eucharist, we sacramentally become transformed into his image.

The Holy Spirit helps us to joyously sing the song of Easter with faith by our words and deeds because, like the soprano and conductor, we know that our Redeemer lives.

Enjoy and share a blessed Easter! Alleluia

4: Seeing Easter Through Children's Eyes

Seeing Easter through children's eyes can open windows of wonder and love that we busy adults sometimes keep closed.

A mother experienced this when she overheard Danny, her five-year old son, talk with his friend Jeremy whose father recently died.

"Where did your dad go when he died?" asked Danny.

"My mom said that he went to Heaven," replied Jeremy.

"What's Heaven?" asked Danny.

Jeremy answered, "My Mom said that Heaven is a place where we go after we die. Everyone will be happy there. We will see Jesus and his mom, grandma and grandpa, your dad, and others we know. I can't wait to go there!"

"Wow! Wow!" exclaimed Danny, "But how did your dad get to Heaven? His jeep is still here."

"I don't know!" replied Jeremy. "I'll ask mom. She knows everything."

Gift of Eternal Life

In their young ways, Jeremy and Danny were struggling to understand the mystery of what happens after death. Later Jeremy's mom explained that on Easter, Christians celebrate Jesus' resurrection, which is the cornerstone of their faith. In First Corinthians 15:14, St. Paul wrote, "If Christ has not been raised, then empty (too) is our preaching; empty, too, your faith."

Christians believe that Christ earned the gift of eternal life for us by his death and resurrection. For those who believe in Christ's resurrection and live their faith, life isn't a dead-end street without an exit but rather the door to eternal life.

Jesus taught us how to love by dying on the cross and offering us the gift of eternal life. He told us to love one another the way he loved us with Easter love.

Loving One Another

On Easter morning a boy walked home through the park. He kept thinking about how the pastor said that Easter love happens when we love each another the way Christ loved us. When we give something to someone who is in need, we really give it to Jesus.

Then he noticed an old man slumped on a park bench. He looked lonely and hungry. The boy sat next to him, took from his pocket a chocolate bar he had been saving, and offered some chocolate to him.

He accepted with a smile. The boy liked his smile so much that, after he had eaten his piece of chocolate, he gave him more. Then they exchanged smiles and sat together in silence.

Finally, the boy got up to leave. As he walked away, he turned, ran back to the bench, and gave the old man a hug and the man gave the boy his best smile.

When the boy arrived home, his mother saw his smile and asked, "What made you so happy today?" He said, "I shared my chocolate bar with Jesus, and he has a great smile!"

Meanwhile the old man returned home smiling. "Why are you so happy," asked his wife? He replied, "Jesus shared a chocolate bar with me. He's much younger than I expected!"

Children need our love, but we also need their love. Perhaps their best gift to us is to call forth our love. In doing so, they remind us that, like Christmas, Easter is about love. May we enjoy an Easter season of love!

5: Easter Reminds Us That the Best is Yet to Come

A widow told her son she sometimes wished that when she died, she could be buried with a fork in her hand. When he asked her why, she explained that at a banquet, the head waitress often requests that we keep our fork because the best is yet to come.

She told her son because of our faith in the resurrection, and God's mercy, that after death the very best is yet to come – the priceless gift of eternal life. Christ's resurrection gives us hope of enjoying eternal happiness in Heaven.

Shock of the Crucifixion

When Christ was crucified on Good Friday, the hopes and dreams of the apostles were crucified with him. They thought that Christ was the Messiah who would drive out the hated Romans.

The shock of the crucifixion was so great that Peter, the leader of the apostles, denied that he knew Christ. He and the apostles ran away and hid because they feared they might be crucified next.

The Risen Lord Appears

Then on the first day of the week, Jesus rose from the dead. The signs of the resurrection were the empty tomb, the burial cloth lying in its folds, and Jesus' appearances. On the same day, Jesus appeared to Mary Magdalene and the other women, to the two disciples on the road to Emmaus, and to the apostles.

But Thomas was absent. A week later the Risen Lord appeared to the apostles again to show them and Thomas that he had risen. In some of his appearances, to show he was not a ghost, he ate with the apostles and invited them to touch him.

Because Jesus rose and appeared to the apostles and others on Sunday, the early Christians replaced the Sabbath with Sunday. The early Christians celebrated the Eucharist with hope and joy on Sunday. Each Sunday became a little Easter.

Gift of Eternal Life

In 1 Corinthians 15:14, St. Paul wrote, "And if Christ has not been raised, then empty (too) is our preaching; empty, too, your faith." By his death and resurrection, Christ overcame sin and death and earned for us the gift of eternal life.

In No. 989 of the Catechism of the Catholic Church, it says, "We firmly believe, and hence we hope that, just as Christ is truly risen from the dead and lives forever, so after death the righteous will live forever with the risen Christ and he will raise them up on the last day."

In No. 1002 of the Catechism of the Catholic Church it says, "Christ will raise us up 'on the last day'; but it is also true that, in a certain way, we have already risen with Christ. For, by virtue of the Holy Spirit, Christian life is already now on earth a participation in the death and Resurrection of Christ.

Already Sharing in The Resurrection

Through Baptism we have been intrinsically changed. Even though we are still subject to this world, nevertheless we spiritually share his resurrection by grace.

But our lives will still be a struggle. To share more fully in the life of the risen Lord, we must daily die to self and daily rise to new life. We must also remember that Jesus can raise us from the death of sin in this life. When we live out our Baptism promises and place ourselves in the hands of Christ and his truth, he can transform us into his witnesses as he did the apostles.

Renewal of Baptismal Promises

The climax of Lent and the Easter vigil is the renewal of our Baptismal promises. Easter gives us hope that, like the widow, the best is yet to be. When we have been faithful to our Baptism promises, after we die, we believe that we will see God face to face in the beatific vision in Heaven. To enjoy the beatific vision in Heaven, we must live a Christ-like life.

Let us rejoice as we renew our Baptismal promises at Easter with deep faith and deepen our commitment to die to sin and rise to new life each day. Enjoy a blessed Easter. Christ has risen. Alleluia!

Chapter Three: Mother's Day

1: How do You Spell Love? M-o-t-h-e-r!

In Isaiah 49:15 Isaiah asks "Can a mother forget her baby, be without tenderness for the child of her womb? Even should she forget, I will never forget you."

This passage praises mothers as symbols of amazing compassion, never forgetting their beloved children. Pope Francis said that a mother is concerned "above all about the health of her children. She cares for them with great and tender love the way Mary, our spiritual, Heavenly mother, cares for us."

History of Mother's Day

Early American attempts to start a Mother's Day began after the Civil War, as a protest to that war's carnage, by women who had lost their sons. This early Mother's Day for peace movement was led by Julia Ward Howe, author of "Battle Hymn of the Republic."

In 1908 Anna Jarvis is credited with starting Mother's Day as we know it. In 1914, President Woodrow Wilson signed the proclamation creating Mother's Day, the second Sunday in May, as a national holiday to honor mothers. This year we celebrate Mother's Day on May 8.

Domestic Church

The Church teaches that each Catholic family is called to be a domestic Church, where parents by their words and deeds teach their children Christian values.

Abraham Lincoln said, "I remember my mother's prayers. They have always followed me and clung to me all my life."

St. John Vianney, the Curé of Ars and patron saint of priests, spoke often of his relationship with his mother. He told his parishioners that virtue passes from the heart of a mother to the heart of her children. He added that his mother created an atmosphere of prayer that she almost breathed into her family's life.

Mothers Teach Us to Pray

Mothers teach us to pray by praying. My mother made sure that we prayed before and after meals. She encouraged us, her children, to pray to discover our vocation. Her prayers helped me to persevere in my vocation.

Our mother taught us to love by loving us. Kate Samperi wrote, "Before becoming a mother, I had a hundred theories on how to raise children. Now I have seven children and only one theory: 'Love them, especially when they least deserve to be loved.'"

A Mother's Love

Rev. Melvin Newland tells of Solomon Rosenberg, his wife, their two sons, and his mother and father who were arrested and sent to a Nazi prison.

The rules were simple. As long as you could work, you were allowed to live. When you became too weak to work, you were exterminated. These were cruel days and human flesh was cheap!

Solomon watched his mother and father marched off to their deaths. He knew that the next victim would be David, his youngest son, who was a frail child.

Every evening Rosenberg returned to the barracks after hours of labor and searched for the faces of his family. When he found them, they huddled together, embraced each another, and thanked God for another day of life.

One day he came back and didn't see those familiar faces. He finally discovered Joshua, his oldest son, huddled in a corner, weeping and praying. He said, "Josh, tell me it's not true!" Joshua replied, "It's true. Today David was not strong enough to do his work. So, they came for him."

"But where's your mother?" asked Mr. Rosenberg, "Oh Poppa," he replied. "When they came for David, he was afraid, and he cried. Momma told him, 'David, there's nothing to be afraid of,' and she took his hand and went with him."

"Can a mother forget her baby?" David's mother answered "Never." She gave David the gift of life; then she gave her life to be with him in his hour of need.

How do you spell love? M-o-t-h-e-r! Wherever our mother is, let's pray that she enjoys a happy Mother's Day!

2: A Good Mother's Love Mirrors God's Love for Us

A Gaelic legend tells of an eagle swooping down and carrying a little baby boy to its lofty nest. The village's strongest men tried to scale the high and rugged cliff, but each one failed. Then to their amazement a small fragile woman climbed the sheer precipice and returned the baby to safety, "How did she do it?", asked the strong men in amazement. She replied proudly, "I am the baby's mother!" A famous mother was asked which of her children she loved the most. She replied, "The child who at the moment needs my love the most at this moment of crisis."

A little boy took a giant step appreciating his mother when he handed her a note he had written. The note read: "For cutting the grass: $5.00: For cleaning my room this week: $1.00, For going to the store for you: $.50 Baby-sitting my kid brother while you went shopping: $3.00, Taking out the garbage: $1.00, For getting a good report card: $5.00, For cleaning up and raking the yard: $2.00, Total owed: $17.50 – in cash please."

His mother turned over the bill he'd written on, and wrote, "For all the nights I carried you while you were growing inside of me: No charge! For all the trying times, and all the tears that you've caused me throughout the years, No charge! For all the nights that I've sat up with you, doctored and prayed for you, No Charge! For all the trying times and all the tears that you've caused through the years: No Charge! For all the nights that were filled with dread, and for the worries I knew were ahead: No Charge! For the toys, food, clothes, and even wiping your nose: No Charge Son. When you add it up, the cost of my love is: No Charge!" When the boy read his mother's note, big tears formed in his eyes. He looked at his mother and said, "Mom, I sure do love you." Then he took the pen and in big letters he wrote: "PAID IN FULL".

An appreciative daughter wrote, "I visit my mom four times a week. On Sundays we go shopping. We are together for two hours. On Mondays and Wednesdays, I bring her lunch and we crochet for an hour. On Saturdays I bring her Communion. That is only a 5-minute stay. I feel guilty that I don't spend more time; and yet, many people tell me I am doing too much. I have a husband, grown children and a grandson in my life and I love my work! God should have put more than 24 hours in a day; of course, if He had, there would be other things to consume my time. Since then her mother has died!

This daughter reminds us that we should honor our mothers not only on Mother's Day but every day whether she is in time or eternity! Let's continue to do so.

3: Mother's Leave Indelible Mark of Love on Our Hearts

A man felt that he was too busy to visit his mother on Mother's Day, so he stopped at a florist to wire her some carnations. A little girl came in and tried to buy a rose for her mom for 75 cents. The clerk told her that a rose costs two dollars. Tears revealed her pain. The man generously paid for the girl's rose and then ordered carnations for his mother.

As he drove thoughtfully away, he saw the little girl in the nearby cemetery. He stopped and saw her tearfully placing the rose on her mother's grave. The man canceled his wire order of carnations. He personally delivered them to his mother. He decided to enjoy her presence while she was still alive.

The "Mother" of Mother's Day

Anna Jarvis (1864-1948) was so proud of her mother that she worked to establish a day when she and others could honor their mother and all mothers. She is known as the "mother" of Mother's Day.

On Mother's Day we honor mothers – living and deceased for their lifelong care, concern, and unconditional love.

Rajneesh, an Indian mystic, said, "The moment a child is born, the mother is also born. She never existed before. The woman existed, but the mother, never. A mother is something absolutely new."

A Mother's Act of Love

An unknown author wrote, "Mothers hold their children's hands for a short while, but their hearts forever." After the events of 9/11, a worried mother phoned her daughter who lived in the area. She discovered that her daughter was safe, but she flew to New York to make sure she was safe by hugging her.

A famous Bible scholar said that the best translation of the Bible was his mother's translation. She translated the Bible into daily acts of love. A sophomore girl I once taught agreed. She wrote, "I can't find anything wrong with my mother. She is kind, forgiving, thoughtful, caring, and patient. She constantly preaches peace in the family. She leads by example."

Peace Begins in the Family

Peace was a major reason for early attempts to establish Mother's Day. A mother told her young children that the best Christmas present they could give her was to stop fighting and give her peace, Peace begins in families.

In No. 2223 of the Catechism of the Catholic Church, it says, "Parents educate their children by creating a home where tenderness, respect, fidelity, and disinterested service are the rule."

Leading by Example

Parents have a responsibility to give a good example to their children. One way to do this is through prayer, Abraham Lincoln said, "I remember my mother's prayers. They have always followed me,"

Every night, my mother knelt and prayed. During Lent, May, and

October, she gathered us for the Rosary like a hen gathers her chicks.

She made sure that we prayed before and after meals. She encouraged us to pray to discover our vocation. Her prayers helped me to persevere in my priesthood. I'm sure she is praying for me in heaven.

The Church encourages mothers to pray to be good mothers. A mother told me, "I'm most proud of being a mother. My grandmothers and mother helped me become the mother I am today. I pray that I can be a good mother like them and pass on their wonderful qualities to my children." I think that she has.

Our Spiritual Mother

On Mother's Day, we also honor Mary, our spiritual mother. When I think of motherhood, I think of Mary.

The Heavenly Father did, too. From all women, he chose Mary to be Jesus' mother. Jesus needed a mother who was full of grace and fully open to God's will to help him grow in wisdom and understanding in his human nature.

A mother wrote that when she first held her baby, she experienced what Mary felt on that first Christmas when she held the Christ child.

During May, we honor her by praying the Rosary, by May crownings, and other devotions.

The morning my Mom died, my brother held her hand and told her that he loved her. Mary told Jesus that she loved him by being under the cross. She was there when Christ needed her.

Mother's Day is a graced day to receive Holy Communion as a family. If our mother has died, we can offer our Communion for her. If she's alive, we can give her a rose, carnation, or a visit. If she has died, like the little girl, we can place a prayer or a rose of love on her grave or pray for her.

4: Mothers are Often Underappreciated

On January 7, 2015, during his general audience, Pope Francis lamented how mothers are often under-appreciated. The pope stated, "To be a mother is a great treasure. Mothers, in their unconditional, sacrificial love for their children, are the antidote to individualism. They are the greatest enemies against war."

Close to Act of Creation

Someone wrote that a mother carries her child in her womb for nine months and in her heart forever. Conceiving, carrying, and giving birth to a human being is as close as any person can come to the act of creation.

Years ago, in a classic Life magazine article entitled "A Woman on Her Way to a Miracle," Eleanor Graves wrote, "Whatever feelings pregnancy may arouse – delight, indifference, resignation, horror – the idea of creating a new human being is awesome!"

"Pregnancy is surely the most creative thing you will ever do, even if done inadvertently. It is hard to believe that at some appointed hour, you will divide like some ancient cell and suddenly it won't be you any longer but you and some other being to whom you will be tied by nerves, tissue, and chemistry all your life."

"This being is already within you, shouting in a sometimes-deafening voice, look out, stand back, here comes a whole new person. You are its lifeline and nourishment. Only you can make sure that its bones are strong, and its eyes are clear. How good you must be, how well behaved, how faithful to this being."

Overwhelming Experience

After giving birth, mothers continue to nurture, sacrifice, love, and ultimately let go of her child or children.

On March 23, according to the Huffington Post, Duchess Kate Middleton, wife of Prince William said, "Nothing can prepare you for the overwhelming experience of what it means to become a mother. It is full of complex emotions of joy, exhaustion, love, and worry all mixed together. "Your fundamental identity changes overnight. You go from thinking of yourself as primarily an individual, to suddenly being a mother, first and foremost."

The Duchess and Prince William are parents of three-year-old George and one-year-old Charlotte.

Mother's Example

St. Jean Vianney, patron saint of priests, said, "Virtues go easily from mothers into their children's hearts. Children often willingly do what they see being done." He added that his mother created an atmosphere of prayer that she almost breathed in her family's life.

My penny-wise mother rarely called us, her children, long-distance when we became adults. However, if she learned that we were sick, she called three or four times a day until she was sure we were okay. Once a mother, always a mother!

Honoring Mothers

Most of us honor our mother every day, but Mother's Day gives us opportunities to honor her in special ways. We can write, call, invite her to dinner, or show our appreciation in other ways. If she is in heaven, we can ask her to hold us in prayer during our personal storms as my mother did.

Mother's Day is a graced time to receive Communion as a family. If our mother cannot participate, we can offer our Communion at Mass for her.

Mothers are the heart of the home. Let's appreciate our mothers now and forever as Jesus did!

5: May Married Couples Pray for the Graces of Marriage

A salvage company organized an expedition to recover treasure from a sunken Spanish treasure ship. Day after day, divers plunged into the cold waters and came up with nothing worthwhile; then, a diver discovered an unexpected treasure that excited the entire crew. It was a wedding ring that a Spanish nobleman gave to his wife. On the ring was a heart with the words, "I have nothing more to give."

These words point to the unconditional love and trust the couple share when they exchange their marriage vows, "I take you to be my (husband/wife.) I promise to be true to you in good times and in bad, in sickness and in health. I will love you and honor you all my life."

Catholics who receive the sacrament of marriage especially treasure their wedding ring because it reminds them daily of the covenant, they made on their wedding day. Since a ring has no beginning or end, it symbolizes the eternal love and unity of the couple.

The late humorist Erma Bombeck wasn't joking when she said, "For years my wedding ring has done its job. It has led me not into temptation. It has reminded my husband numerous times at parties that it's time to go home. It has been a source of relief to a dinner companion. It has been a status symbol in the maternity ward."

Fr. Walter Burghardt said that Catholic marriage is too serious to be left solely to husband and wife. In marriage, husband and wife are united to each other with Jesus in marriage. In No. 1660 of the Catechism of the Catholic Church it says, "Christ the Lord raised marriage between the baptized to the dignity of a sacrament." Jesus helps the couple live this sacrament through special graces when the cold North wind of worry begins to blow or when the lamp of love flickers low. A daily communicant who experienced a difficult marriage surprised her pastor when she exclaimed, "Father, on your wedding day, you don't see the stations of the cross." Even in a good marriage there may be unexpected crosses such as death, severe illness and other unexpected setbacks. Christ can give the couple strength to do what they cannot do by themselves.

In No. 1642 of the Catechism of the Catholic Church it says, "Christ dwells with the couple, gives them the strength to take up their crosses and follow him, to rise after they have fallen, to forgive one another, to bear one another's burdens, and to love one another with supernatural, tender, and fruitful love." By responding to the graces of marriage, the couple help each other to attain holiness in their marriage and welcome and educate their children.

In Catholic marriage husband and wife are called to love each other as Christ loves the Church. Marriage is the school of love because the couple learn to love more deeply as they grow together. Husband and wife are called to sacrifice for each other and for their children.

Sacrificial love involves giving and receiving. It may be as simple as laying down the newspaper when the other wishes to communicate. It may involve cooking a special meal with love, doing one's share, or giving encouragement when the cold north wind of worry blows, or the lamp of hope dims low. After coming home, my niece would ask: "Dad, were you good to mom today?"

Sacrificial love may be as complicated as postponing one's career in order to give more quality time to the children. It can mean lying awake nights because the baby is teething or missing one's favorite television program repeatedly to attend a school play or child's soccer game. It may mean supporting the other during an illness. Spouses are career students in the school of love. They never stop learning to love, forgive, and grow. I rejoice when I hear a married person say, "My spouse is my best friend" or "My spouse is Christ to me!"

In the Church, marriage is a sacrament. In No. 1603 of the Catechism of the Catholic Church it says, "Marriage is not a human institution despite the many variations it may have undergone through the centuries in different cultures, social structures and spiritual attitudes in marriage. Both are united in an unbreakable bond."

Fr. William Bausch once playfully, but seriously; wrote that a Catholic couple will surely get to Heaven because the corporal and spiritual works of mercy are built into their marriage. The couple feed the hungry, give drink to the thirsty, comfort the sorrowful and instruct the unlearned.

One of my favorite examples of married love begins with the question: "Can anything be more beautiful than young love?" Someone answered, "Yes, it's an old married couple finishing their life's journey together. Their hands are gnarled, but still clasped; their faces are wrinkled but still radiant; their hearts are physically tired, but still strong with love and devotion for one another." Amen!

Chapter Four: Earth Day

1: Let's Make Every Day an Earth Day

We in Wisconsin should especially appreciate Earth Day because it was started by Gaylord Nelson when he was a U.S. senator from Wisconsin.

On April 22, 1970, 20 million Americans crowded streets, parks, and auditoriums to celebrate the first Earth Day. They called for a healthy, sustainable environment. Earth Days' time had come.

Respecting the Earth

I learned to respect Earth Day and the environment from my dad's example. He usually planted and cared for a garden. In early spring, when it was still cold, he grew plants in a glass covered structure heated by fermented manure called a "hot bed". It protected the young plants from the cold.

Dad's example motivated me to choose conservation as my 4H project. In seventh and eighth grade, our class also studied from a supplementary textbook on agriculture that included conservation.

At Platteville University, I took a course in conservation; consequently, when ecology was discussed in the seminary, I had a fresh start on my urban classmates. Many of them had never heard of ecology.

Ecology and Morality

St. Francis of Assisi is the patron saint of ecology because he loved God's creation. Recent popes have emphasized that ecology is related to human morality. In his 2016 encyclical *Laudato Si' (On Care of our Common Home)*, Pope Francis wrote that humans must care for creation and share its fruits with one another, especially the poor, through little daily actions. He said education can bring about changes in lifestyle.

At Beloit Catholic High in the 1980s, we celebrated an Earth Day service which in some ways embodied Pope Francis' words. The service arose from a conversation between our biology teacher, our principal, and me. This prayer service involved faculty, students, and others.

Rainbow of Hope

We decided to use a rainbow image in our prayer service because rainbows symbolize hope and beauty. Just as different colors contribute to a rainbow's beauty, so too each of us has different gifts that we can contribute to a healthy, beautiful environment.

We began by drawing the outline of a large rainbow on the floor. Then we taped pieces of poster cardboard together and cut the cardboard in the shape of the rainbow outline we drew on the floor. We colored the pieces of cardboard with the colors of a rainbow. We cut the cardboard rainbow into pieces and gave each piece to a homeroom. We colored the pieces of cardboard with the colors of the rainbow. We cut the cardboard rainbow into pieces and gave each piece to a homeroom.

Each homeroom suggested three or more ways they could improve the local environment. They wrote these ways on their piece of the cardboard rainbow.

Practical Ideas

At the prayer service, homeroom representatives shared ways that they would respect and improve the environment. They wrote their ways on their piece of rainbow. Each piece of rainbow with its homeroom commitments was taped with carpet tape to the outline drawn on bright white paper stapled to a large portable platform. Piece by piece a rainbow of hope gradually appeared.

Some practical ways that we shared to keep earth bright and beautiful included: 1) plant a tree, 2) become informed on ways to improve the environment, 3) plant and care for a garden, 4) recycle, 5) participate in highway litter pickup, 6) pick up litter and set an example, 7) walk or ride a bike if we can instead of driving.

Earth Day has made Americans more aware of the blessings and beauty of the environment. Pope Francis reminds us that earth is our common home and mother. She provides food, clothing, shelter, water, beauty, and much more! Let's continue to be informed and do our part to keep the environment neat, clean, and healthy. Let's make every day an Earth Day!

2: Making Each Day an Earth Day

For some astronauts, an unexpected result of their participation in the space program was a deepening of their faith in God.

Frank Borman was commander of the first space crew to travel beyond Earth's orbit. Looking down on Earth from 250,000 miles away, he radioed back a message, quoting Genesis 1: "In the beginning, God created the Heavens and the earth." He later added, "After viewing Earth from space, I experienced an enormous feeling that there had to be a power greater than any of us, that there was a God and a beginning."

Astronaut John Glenn exclaimed, "To look out at creation from space and not believe in God is, to me, impossible."

Reminds Us of God's Presence

Our vast universe, the mini universe of a cell, and creation's other marvels can open us to God's presence as it did for these and other astronauts. Earth nourishes us physically by providing food, clothing, and shelter. Creation feeds our hunger for beauty with flowers, sun, moon, stars, and God's other endless masterpieces.

In Psalm 19: 1-2 it says, "The Heavens declare God's glory, the skies proclaim the handiwork of God's hands. Day after day they pour forth speech; night after night they reveal knowledge."

St. Athanasius wrote, "The firmament with its magnificence, beauty, and order is an admirable preacher of its Maker, whose eloquence fills the universe."

In No. 341 of the Catechism of the Catholic Church, it says, "Creation's beauty reflects the Creator's infinite beauty and ought to inspire the respect and submission of man's intellect and will." St. John Paul II said, "Creation remains kind of a first revelation which speaks to us clearly of the Creator and can lead us ever more deeply into the mystery of God's love for us."

Safeguarding the Earth

In his 2015 Earth Day Message, Pope Francis stated, "The Earth is an environment to be safeguarded, a garden to be cultivated. The relationship of mankind with nature must not be conducted with greed, manipulation, and exploitation, but it must conserve the divine harmony that exists between creatures and creation within the logic of respect and care, so it can be put to the service of our brothers, also of future generations."

Pope Benedict XVI fears that we are losing the attitude of wonder and contemplation by not listening to creation.

In his Memoirs, the Venerable Fr. Mazzuchelli wrote, "How beautiful and sublime are thoughts that come to one who, lying on the vast meadow, was led by countless glowing stars to contemplate the glory of God.

"If God provides for his servants a room so rich as to contemplate in the silence of the night, who could imagine what He has prepared for their enjoyment in the eternal and most radiant day of paradise.

"I believe that King David, St. Patrick, and other shepherds and saints came closer to God by contemplating God's heavenly cities of stars at night."

Wonders of Spring

We in the Midwest are graced because after winter, green grass rises from its winter tomb and flowers again delight us as stars of earth. Birds happily sing their alleluias of joy, crickets chirp, and guided by

God, geese honk in squadron flight.

The joy of risen life echoes in happy energetic sounds of playing children. Couples walk hand in hand as their eyes glow with love! First Communions, proms, and Pentecost invite us to enjoy Christ's loving risen beauty.

To enjoy and be renewed by nature's wonder and beauty, each year millions of Americans retreat to woods, water, and nature to relax and get in touch with their inner self. Contact with nature resurrects the mystic in us, feeds our hunger for beauty, and can help bring us closer to God as it did for some astronauts.

Celebrating Earth Day

We celebrate Earth Day on Friday, April 22, this year. Earth Day was started by Wisconsin Senator Gaylord Nelson to teach us to take better care of the environment.

He declared, "The battle to restore a proper relationship between man and his environment and between man and other living creatures requires a long, sustained political, moral, ethical, and financial commitment, far beyond any effort made before."

We can make each day an Earth Day by responsible recycling, using renewable energy at home and work, and asking elected officials to vote for responsible legislation that helps and heals the environment. If we're able, we can plant trees, walk, ride a bike, or participate in other activities.

A precious gift we can give to future generations is to work together to care for Mother Earth so they can enjoy her blessings as much or more than we do.

3: Earth Day Seeks to Protect and Save All Species

The theme of earth day is to protect and save all species. Earth Day was founded by Wisconsin Senator Gaylord Nelson. He witnessed the devastation caused by an enormous oil spill in Santa Barbara, Calif., which hurt the environment.

In 1969, he proposed the idea to celebrate Earth Day. As always, this year's Earth Day occurs on April 22, the day after we celebrate the resurrection of Jesus.

Upsetting the Balance of Nature

According to the Earth Day Network, "Nature's gifts to our planet are the millions of species that we know and love, and many more that remain to be discovered. Unfortunately, human beings have irrevocably upset the balance of nature and, as a result, the world is facing the greatest rate of extinction since the loss of dinosaurs more than 60 million years ago.

"Unlike the dinosaurs' fate, the rapid extinction of species in our world today is the result of human activity. The unprecedented global destruction and rapid reduction of plant and wildlife populations are directly linked to causes driven by human activity: climate change, deforestation, habitat loss, trafficking and poaching, unsustainable agriculture, pollution, and pesticides, to name a few. The impacts are far reaching."

Pope Focuses on Ecology

When Cardinal Jorge Maria Bergoglio became pope, he chose the papal name of Francis of Assisi, the patron saint of ecology. By doing so, he signaled that his pontificate would have a particular focus upon environmental issues and continue what Pope John Paul II, Pope Benedict, and Church teaching has supported.

Pope Francis supports many of the ideas of Earth Day. In his first papal homily, Pope Francis urged the faithful to protect the earth just as St. Joseph protected the Christ Child.

On May 24, 2015, Pope Francis promulgated the landmark encyclical Laudate Si'. He stated that St. Francis of Assisi reminds us that our common home is like a sister with whom we share our life and a mother who opens her arms to embrace us.

In numbers 33-34 of Laudate Si', Pope Francis stated, "Each year sees the disappearance of thousands of plant and animal species which we will never know, which our children will never see. The great majority become extinct for reasons related to human activity. Because of us, thousands of species will no longer give glory to God by their very existence, nor convey their message to us. We have no such right.

"The good functioning of ecosystems also requires fungi, algae, worms, insects, reptiles, and an innumerable variety of microorganisms. Some less numerous species, although generally unseen, nonetheless play a critical role in maintaining the equilibrium of a particular place. Human beings must intervene when a geosystem reaches a critical state."

In number's 38 and 40 of Laudate Si', the pope also calls the Amazon and the Congo basin the "lungs of our planet." On oceans he writes, "Oceans not only contain the bulk of our planet's water supply, but also most of the immense variety of living creatures, many of them still unknown to us and threatened for various reasons."

Pope Francis also notes, "The social dimensions of global change include the effects of technological innovations on employment, social exclusion, an inequitable distribution and consumption of energy and other services, social breakdown, increased violence, and a rise in new forms of social aggression, drug trafficking, growing drug use by young people, and the loss of identity."

The pope wrote, "Today, however, we have to realize that a true ecological approach always becomes a social approach; it must integrate questions of justice in debates on the environment, so as to hear both the cry of the earth and the cry of the poor."

Good News

The good news is that the rate of extinctions can still be slowed, and many of our declining, threatened, and endangered species can still recover if we together vow to build a united global movement of consumers, voters, educators, faith leaders, and scientists to demand immediate action.

Earth Day Network is asking people to join its Protect our Species campaign to educate and raise awareness about the accelerating rate of extinction of millions of species and the causes and consequences of this phenomenon; achieve major policy victories that protect broad groups of species as well as individual species and their habitats; build and activate a global movement that embraces nature and its values; and encourage individual actions such as adopting plant-based diet and stopping pesticide and herbicide use.

4: Earth Day Invites Us To Care for Our Home on Earth

I gratefully recall the evening when Dad and I sat on our front lawn and studied the farmer's green field across the road. The sun like a beautiful orange-red host sank slowly into the chalice of God's good earth. It was a heavenly moment of harmony between God, nature, Dad, and me.

The Earth is God's

Dad broke the sacred silence by saying, "You know, we don't really own anything!" During the silence that followed, I visualized the deed to our land. In my imagination, owner after owner paraded across its pages.

Dad was right. God owns the land. We are earth's temporary caretakers. When we die, the land we temporarily own passes on to others.

In Psalm 24, it says, "The Earth is God's and all that is in it, the world and all who dwell therein."

We Are Stewards of the Land

In Genesis, it says that God created men and women and made them stewards of the land. Scripture reveals that we cannot be in a right relationship with God unless we are in a right relationship with the land.

The Hebrews believed the "land" meant the ground, the trees and plants, the rivers and seas, the animals, and all other human beings, even the air we breathe. An astonishing world of beauty and plenty for all is God's temporary loan for us to enjoy.

Caring for the Earth

We celebrate Earth Day on April 22. It was started by Wisconsin Senator Gaylord Nelson to teach and to inspire us to better care for the environment. Over one billion persons in 192 countries now take part in it.

Senator Nelson declared: "The battle to restore a proper relationship between man and his environment and other living creatures will require a long, sustained, political, moral, ethical, and financial commitment, far beyond any effort made before." He was a prophet!

In his 2015 Earth Day Message, Pope Francis stated, "The Earth is an environment to be safeguarded, a garden to be cultivated. The relationship of mankind with nature must not be conducted with greed, manipulation, and exploitation, but it must conserve the divine harmony that exists between creatures and creation within the logic of respect and care, so it can be put to the service of our brothers, sisters, and future generations."

The Venerable Father Samuel Mazzuchelli, who served in Iowa, Michigan, Illinois, and Wisconsin, including our diocese, respected creation. Creation helped him to feel closer to God.

In her book, Samuel Mazzuchelli, American Dominican, Sr. Mary Nona McGreal wrote, "Landscaping was one of Father Mazzuchelli's Italian gifts. At Sinsinawa Mound and Benton, the land was barren because of extensive mining. In both places, he planted trees to beautify the land, prevent erosion, and help provide other benefits." In these and other ways, he practiced good ecology.

St. Francis of Assisi, whose name Pope Francis took, is the patron saint of ecology. He loved God's creation. So does Pope Francis. In 2016 Pope Francis wrote a groundbreaking encyclical on creation entitled Laudato Si' (On Care of our Common Home). Our pope wrote that we humans must care for creation and share its fruits with one another, especially the poor, through little daily actions.

Celebrating Earth Day

We can join the Earth Day network as an individual or group. We can take the St. Francis Pledge to Care for Creation and the Poor,

If we are able, we can plant trees, walk, or ride a bike. We can recycle, use renewable energy at home and work. We can become better informed about the Church's teaching regarding the environment and teach the young to do the same. We can keep practicing good habits of ecology.

Earth Day's 2018 theme is "End Plastic Pollution." This is a problem Father Mazzuchelli did not have to face. According to the 2018 Earth Day organizers, plastic pollution is not just an environmental crisis, but an urgent public health, human rights, and social justice issue.

It poisons marine life, disrupts human hormones, litters our beaches, and clogs our streams. Inspired by the ecology movement, highway pickup was an almost immediate success, but ending plastics pollution will take longer. For this reason, it is part of a five-year effort that began in 2016, builds up to the 50th anniversary of Earth Day in 2020, and continues for the next decade.

The End Plastic Pollution campaign includes three key components: educating citizens to help them change their behaviors and those of their communities; engaging business leaders to establish new commitments to reduce and eliminate plastic pollution; and working with governments to build support for a global framework to prevent and manage plastic pollution.

As Dad taught me, we don't own the earth. God does. We are its temporary stewards. When we respect, care for, and work with creation, we respect God.

Let us make each day an Earth Day so we can help future generations enjoy creation's blessings as much or more than we do. Together, we can do it!

Chapter Five: Memorial Day

1: Remembering Those Who died for Our Country

Memorial Day is a federal holiday observed on the last Monday of May. On Memorial Day we honor military personnel who died while serving our country, particularly those who died in battle or from wounds sustained in battle.

On Veterans Day, we honor those who served honorably in military service during wartime or peacetime. Memorial Day began as Decoration Day, which originated after the American Civil War to remember the Union and Confederate soldiers who died in that war. Eventually Memorial Day was extended to honor all American military personnel who died in combat.

Just War Theory

Jesus came to bring peace. In Matt. 26:51-52, when the soldiers came to seize Jesus, it says, "One of those who followed Jesus drew his sword and cut off the ear of the high priest's servant." Jesus ordered, "Put your sword back in its sheath. For all who take the sword will perish by the sword."

Early Christians did not bear arms. When Christ didn't come a second time to bring peace, some Christians concluded that sometimes it was necessary to fight to keep evil people from exploiting the weak and innocent.

St. Augustine formulated the Just War theory which reluctantly permits war when certain conditions are met. War must be a last resort after all other means have been ineffective, be waged for a just cause by legitimate authority, have reasonable hope of success, and intend to achieve peace.

A soldier who was a Japanese POW for three years and survived the Bataan death march explained, "War is always horrible, even when you're on the side of good and battling evil. Killing another human or holding a fallen comrade in your arms is never easy." Some say that war never decides who is right, but only who is left.

Heroic Sacrifices

Despite war's darkness, military personnel sometimes make heroic sacrifices. During the Korean War, Richard Manning and Ray Brennan were in a foxhole. A grenade unexpectedly landed next to Ray Brennan. Brennan jumped on it and died so his friend could live.

Eight years later Manning entered the Franciscan priesthood. Because of his friend's sacrifice, he took the name Brennan as his first name, as customary for Religious orders. He hoped to live sacrificially as his friend who died for him had lived.

Agents of Security and Freedom

In No. 79 of the Pastoral Constitution of the Church in the Modern World, it says "Those who devote themselves to the military service of their country should regard themselves as agents of security and freedom of peoples. As long as they fulfill this role properly, they are making a genuine contribution to the establishment of peace."

Many enter military service because they desire to protect their homeland's freedom and security.

Military personnel sacrifice time, plans, comfort, and sometimes their lives so that we might live in freedom and peace; however, earthly peace is fragile.

President Dwight Eisenhower said, "Though force can protect us in emergencies, only justice, fairness, consideration, and cooperation can finally lead humanity to the dawn of eternal peace."

God's Plan of Peace

Isaiah 2:4 expresses God's plan of peace, "They shall beat their swords into ploughshares, and their spears into pruning-hooks, nation shall not lift up sword against nation, neither shall they learn war anymore."

War should motivate us to work for peace and for ordering society according to God's plan, not man's plan.

At Mass we pray for God's gift of peace. Before we receive Communion, we reverently pray the prayer based upon some words of the centurion-soldier, "Lord, I am not worthy that you should enter under my roof, but only say the word and my soul shall be healed."

May the Eucharist strengthen us to bring peace to our homes, neighborhoods, work, and world.

2: Memorial Day Reminds Us to Work for Peace

In Vietnam, Brian Rooney, an Army medic, knelt to read a dying soldier's dog tags. As he did, the soldier whispered, "Remember me." Rooney promised that he would remember him.

He certainly did. According to the May 23, 2003, *Los Angeles Daily News*, Brian Rooney spent thousands of his dollars and hundreds of hours memorializing and remembering America's war dead.

Memorial Day

Memorial Day is a federal holiday when we join Rooney in remembering military men and women who died while serving our country. In 1868, General John A. Logan, commander-in-chief of the Grand Army of the Republic, named May 30 as a special day to honor Union soldiers' graves by strewing them with flowers or otherwise decorating the graves of soldiers who died during the Civil War, it was appropriately called Decoration Day.

By the 20th Century, competing Union and Confederate traditions honoring Civil War veterans had merged. Gradually Decoration Day became known as Memorial Day and was expanded to honor all Americans who died in military service.

In 1971, Memorial Day was declared a national holiday by an Act of Congress. Its date was moved from May 30 to the last Monday in May to extend the weekend. Some claim this change made it easier to be distracted from Memorial Day's meaning. They advocate returning it to May 30 to keep its true meaning.

Following the Prince of Peace

Because they followed Christ, the Prince of Peace, early Christians didn't bear arms. When Christ didn't come a second time to bring peace, some Christians concluded that sometimes it was necessary to fight to keep evil people from forcing their will on weak, innocent people.

Consequently, St. Augustine formulated the Just War Theory, which reluctantly permits war when the following rigorous conditions are met: War should be a last resort for a just cause by legitimate grave, and certain, have serious prospects of success, and the use of arms must not produce evils and disorders graver than the evil to be eliminated"

We Christians are urged to join others in working for peace. In 2317 of the *Catechism of the Catholic Church*, it says, "Injustice, excessive economic or social inequalities, envy, distrust, and pride raging among men and nations constantly threaten peace and cause wars. Everything done to overcome these disorders contributes to building peace and avoiding war."

Chaplain Died Helping Others

In the 1941 surprise attack on Pearl Harbor, the battleship U.S.S. Oklahoma was sunk by aerial torpedoes. Fr. Aloysius Schmitt of the Archdiocese of Dubuque died while helping to save 12 shipmates by lifting them through a small porthole. He was the first chaplain killed during World War II.

On September 8, 2016, the remains of Father Schmitt were identified. A service was held in his hometown of St. Lucas, Iowa, on October 5. His remains were interred at Loras College on October 8

In *Pacem in Terris*, Pope St. John XXIII wrote, "So magnificent is this aim (for peace) that human resources alone, though inspired by the most praiseworthy good will, cannot hope to achieve it. God must come to man's aid with his Heavenly assistance if human society is to bear the closest possible resemblance to the kingdom of God."

Let's pray for and remember those who died for our country. Let's also pray for innocent victims of war and continue to be Christ's instruments who work for peace.

3: Let's Remember Chaplains on Memorial Day

In 1953 Fr. Emil Kapaun, an Army chaplain died as a prisoner of war during the Korean War. St. John Paul II honored him with the title of "Servant of God," the first step on the path towards sainthood.

On April 11, 2013, President Barack Obama presented him with the Congressional Medal of Honor "for bravery above and beyond the call of duty." He is the ninth military chaplain to receive this honor.

President Obama described him as a soldier who didn't bear a gun, but who wielded the mightiest weapon of all – a love for his brothers so pure that he was willing to die so that they might live!

When his unit was attacked by Chinese Communist forces, Father Kapaun calmly walked through deadly enemy fire to provide medical aid and comforting words. He gave the last rites to wounded Catholics. When Father Kapaun saw a Chinese soldier about to execute Father's wounded comrade, Sergeant First Class Herbert A. Miller, he rushed to push the gun away and saved his life. He carried him many miles to a prison camp.

Mr. Miller attended the White House ceremony when Father Kapaun was honored with the Medal of Honor.

Through the winter as prisoners froze to death, Father Kapaun offered them his clothes, sneaked out to bring them grain, and cleaned prisoner's wounds. Guards tortured him for his courageous faith, but on Easter they looked on as he offered Mass.

Examples of Bravery

The four chaplains on the S.S. Dorchester are another example of heroic bravery. They were Rev. George L. Fox, a Methodist minister; Rabbi Alexander D. Goode; Rev. John P. Washington, a Catholic priest; and Rev. Clark V. Poling, a Reformed Church of America minister.

On February 3, 1943, a Nazi submarine torpedoed the S.S. *Dorcheste*r in the cold North Atlantic waters near Greenland. More than 900 Americans were aboard the ship. Nearly 700 men died. The chaplains moved about the ship, handing out life jackets and helping injured soldiers toward lifeboats.

When the order came to abandon ship, the chaplains gave their life jackets to four soldiers. Then, they locked their arms, folded their hands in prayer, and went down together with their ship. Their heroic actions were a sign of unity for which Jesus prayed.

Appreciating Chaplains

During my four years of active duty in the U. S. Navy, I appreciated the chaplains who served where I was stationed.

At the San Diego Naval station, when I went to Confession, the zealous chaplain asked me if I ever considered priesthood. Later at Sunday Masses in 1954, he introduced worshippers to the dialogue Mass which prepared Catholics for the full, conscious, and active participation which the Second Vatican Council encouraged.

When I was assigned to the USS Hamel, a flagship and Destroyer Tender, our chaplain was a minister who held protestant services. When we were in port, boats were always available to take Catholics to Masses, which were offered within a reasonable distance.

I remember when I was the only Catholic who requested to go to Mass. I was informed that no boat was available. Our first-class petty officer was not a very religious person, but he raised the roof in protest. I suspect too that this was a rare chance to show his authority. Thanks to him, we both felt important as one boat came for me.

Eventually a Catholic priest was assigned to our ship as chaplain. We now had the opportunity for daily and Sunday Mass. I began to serve Mass and asked if we might have a retreat. After the retreat, the chaplain asked me to consider priesthood. He influenced my journey to priesthood.

The Responsibilities

Military chaplains are responsible for the religious and moral well-being of service members and their families. The chaplain's responsibilities include everything from performing religious rites and conducting worship services to providing counseling and advising commanders on religious, spiritual, and moral matters.

Military chaplains perform other duties, beyond the expertise of this poor writer that only a military chaplain can fully describe. May we honor and pray for all military men and women who served our country, including military chaplains.

VI: SUMMER

Chapter One: Summer Feasts

1: Important Feasts That Prepare Us for a Heavenly Summer

Each year, we celebrate four of the most important feasts of the Church on four consecutive Sundays in our diocese. These feasts are Ascension, Pentecost, the Solemnity of the Body and Blood of Christ and the Blessed Trinity. Like cars on a freeway during rush hour, they come quickly one after another. This rapidity of feasts during a busy time of graduations, weddings, vacations and other activities may hinder us from fully enjoying their graces.

In 2019 we celebrated the Ascension of Jesus into Heaven on June 2. The Ascension is not so much about Jesus' absence, but his being present in a new way. Jesus has not abandoned us or left us orphans, but he intercedes for us from Heaven. From Heaven Jesus sent the Holy Spirit at Pentecost to help us be his witnesses wherever we are.

The same year we celebrated Pentecost on June 9th. Pentecost has been called the birthday of the Catholic Church when the early church came of age. The apostles received the Holy Spirit on Easter evening. The wider Church received the Holy Spirit on Pentecost when Mary was also present. On Pentecost Peter and the apostles who deserted Jesus on Good Friday were transformed into courageous witnesses of Christ. The Church spread rapidly from Jerusalem to Samaria to the earth's ends. During Confirmation we receive the Holy Spirit whom the church received at Pentecost to strengthen us to be his witnesses as the apostles were.

On June 16, we celebrated the feast of the Most Holy Trinity, the feast of God. The faith of us Christians rests on the Trinity. We were baptized in the name of the Father, Son and Holy Spirit. We begin and end Mass with the sign of the cross in the name of the Father, Son and Holy Spirit. During Mass the priest leads us in prayer to the Father through Jesus in the Holy Spirit.

In No. 234 of the Catechism of the Catholic Church it says, "The mystery of the Most Holy Trinity is the central mystery of Christian faith and life. It is the mystery of God in Himself. The whole history of salvation is identical with the history of the way and means by which the one true Father, Son and Holy Spirit reveals himself to men, and reconciles and unites with himself those who turn away from sin."

In No. 2205 of the Catechism of the Catholic Church, it says that the family is a communion of persons, a sign and image of the communion of the Father and the Son in the Holy Spirit. In the procreation and education of children, it reflects the Father's work of creation. The family is called to partake of Christ's prayer and sacrifice. Daily prayer and the reading of God's word strengthen them in charity. The Christian family has an evangelizing task.

Finally, in 2019 on June 23rd, we celebrated the Feast of the Body and Blood of Christ. In the 13th century St. Juliana of Mont Cornillon, a Belgian nun, experienced a vision of the moon with a dark spot. Jesus revealed to her that the dark spot indicated that the Church needed a separate feast of the Eucharist. The Church already celebrated the institution of the Eucharist on Holy Thursday; but, Holy Thursday points to Jesus' passion and death and begins the Easter Triduum. Through Sister Juliana's efforts, in 1264 Pope Urban IV commanded that the feast of Corpus Christi be observed by the Universal Church.

Corpus Christi focuses upon adoration and belief in the Real Presence. In No. 1418 of The Catechism of the Catholic Church it says, "Because Christ is present in the sacrament of the altar, he is to be honored with the worship of adoration. To visit the Blessed Sacrament is a proof of gratitude, an expression of love, and a duty of adoration towards Christ our Lord."

To receive Communion worthily we must recognize that we are receiving Christ. Eucharistic adoration and the Mass offer opportunities to recognize and adore Jesus in the Eucharist. When we receive Communion, the priest, deacon or extra-ordinary minister holds up the host and says, "the Body of Christ." We respond by saying "Amen" which means I believe that I am receiving Christ. We receive Christ to strengthen us to become a more Christ like person.

To summarize, within a few weeks, we celebrate the feast of the

Ascension of Christ into Heaven where he intercedes for us and sent the Holy Spirit to strengthen us to be his witnesses which we celebrate at Pentecost. The next Sunday we celebrate the feast of the Most Holy Trinity, the feast of God. The following Sunday we celebrate the feast of the Body and Blood of Christ.

Recognizing the Real Presence of Christ in the Eucharist helps us to receive him more fruitfully. These feasts can help prepare us for summer and for Eternity.

2: Pentecost Reminds Us to Use Gifts of Holy Spirit

I was confirmed in seventh grade. In religion class, I learned that in the Sacrament of Confirmation we receive the Holy Spirit who strengthens us to be Christian witnesses. I worried whether I could witness to Christ by dying for him as a martyr. I took Confirmation seriously.

The Church received the Holy Spirit at Pentecost. To prepare to receive the Spirit, for nine days key followers of Jesus gathered in the Upper Room in Jerusalem. These included the apostles, together with Mary, some other women, and disciples. They were united in intense prayer.

In Acts 2:2-4, it says, "Suddenly there came from the sky, a noise like a strong driving wind, and it filled the entire house in which they were. Tongues as of fire appeared to them, which parted and came to rest on each one of them. And they were all filled with the Holy Spirit and began to speak in different tongues, as the Spirit enabled them to proclaim."

Transformed by the Spirit

At the sounds from the Upper Room, a crowd gathered. Peter with the 11 testified to them that the Spirit had come down upon them as Jesus promised. In Acts 2:37-38, it says, "The people were moved by Peter's words. They asked, 'What are we to do?'

"Peter replied, 'Repent and be baptized, every one of you in the name of Jesus Christ, and you will receive the gift of the Holy Spirit.'" As a result, about 3,000 persons were added to their number that day. This is why some call Pentecost the birthday of the Church.

When the Apostles received the Holy Spirit, they were changed from frightened and confused followers into courageous witnesses of Jesus. All except John died for Christ.

Strengthened by the Holy Spirit, despite persecution, the Church quickly spread throughout the Roman Empire. In 313, Constantine issued the Edict of Milan, which established religious toleration for Christianity and all religions in the Roman Empire.

Instruments of Christ's Mission

At Confirmation, we received the gifts and fruits of the Holy Spirit. As witnesses of Christ, we probably won't be called to be martyrs for Christ. But the Holy Spirit empowers us to do our small but important part to help to change this world into a more Christ-like place.

Catholic laity have important roles as Christian witnesses. They are the ordinary point of the Church's contact with the world and the primary instruments of Christ's mission there. The Spirit helps them to influence society, family, culture, art, and other areas of life in their families, neighborhood, work, and society.

In No. 31 of Lumen Gentium it says, "The laity live in the world, that is, in each and in all of the secular professions and occupations. They live in the ordinary circumstances of family and social life. They are called there by God that by exercising their proper function and led by the spirit of the Gospel they may work for the sanctification of the world from within as a leaven."

To help them do this, confirmed Catholics need virtues such as honesty, justice, sincerity, kindness, and courage.

Committed lay Catholics influence the common good by voting responsibly, asking accountability from elected representatives, and making sure government policies protect God-given human dignity and rights.

Being Responsible Catholic Parents

Married Catholic laypersons deeply influence Church and society by being responsible parents. Children are the hope of the future. The best gift parents can give their children is to love each other and their children. Children learn how to love by being loved.

In No. 2223 of the Catechism of the Catholic Church, it says. "Parents have a grave responsibility to give good example to their children." Responsible parents model love, forgiveness. peace, and respect for marriage's sanctity. They teach their children respect for life from the womb to tomb.

Opening Ourselves to God's Will

Mary, the first and greatest Christian, is "God's Masterpiece." She lived a life filled with family concerns and labors. She witnessed to Jesus by being fully open to God's will, following her son to the cross, Mary prayed with the Church at Pentecost.

Pentecost reminds us to take our Confirmation seriously. Let us ask the Spirit to help us follow Jesus and be open to God's will like Mary. May the Holy Spirit help us to continue to be Christ-like witnesses where we live, work, recreate, or wherever we are.

Feast of Corpus Christi: Celebrating Real Presence of Christ in Eucharist

Each year we celebrate Corpus Christi, the feast of the Eucharist. In Latin Corpus Christi means the Body of Christ. The full Latin name of this feast is "Corpus et Sanguis Christi" – "The Body and Blood of Christ."

In some countries and sometimes in our diocese, during this feast there are edifying processions when the sacred host is carried outdoors or around the church.

Unique Gift of the Eucharist

In the 13th century Sister Juliana of Mont-Cornillon, an Augustinian Belgian nun, experienced a vision of the moon with a dark spot. Jesus revealed to her that the dark spot indicated that the Church needed a feast of the Eucharist.

The Church already celebrated the institution of the Eucharist on Holy Thursday, But Holy Thursday centers on Jesus' passion and death and begins the Easter Triduum. She was instructed in her vision to plead that the Church establish the feast of Corpus Christi to focus upon Jesus' unique gift of the Eucharist.

On the feast of Corpus Christi, we honor the Real Presence of Christ in the Eucharist, the great Sacrament. This feast reminds us that Jesus is present in a special sacramental way in the Eucharistic species.

Receiving Christ's Body and Blood

In No. 1413 of the Catechism of the Catholic Church it says, "By the consecration the transubstantiation of the bread and wine into the Body and Blood of Christ is brought about. Under the consecrated species of bread and wine Christ himself, living and glorious, is present in a true, real, and substantial manner: his Body and his Blood, with his soul and his divinity."

During Mass at the Consecration and the Lamb of God, the priest holds up the consecrated host for us to recognize and adore. This prepares us to receive Christ more worthily.

When the bishop, priest, or deacon holds up the Body of Christ at Communion, we respond "Amen" which means we believe in the Real Presence.

Importance of Eucharistic Adoration

Eucharistic Adoration outside Mass increased when the early Church started reserving the host for the sick. In No. 1418 of the Catechism of the Catholic Church, it says, "Because Christ himself is present in the sacrament of the altar, he is to be honored with the worship of Adoration. To visit the Blessed Sacrament is a proof of gratitude, an expression of love, and a duty of adoration toward Christ our Lord."

Archbishop Fulton Sheen constantly promoted prayer before the Blessed Sacrament. He said, "We become like that upon which we gaze. Looking at the Eucharistic Lord for an hour transforms our heart in mysterious ways."

For him, Adoration was like an oxygen tank that revived the Holy Spirit's breath in us. He preached that Eucharistic Adoration fosters vocations and transforms individuals and dioceses.

Receiving Communion

Eucharistic Adoration increases our desire to receive Christ in the Eucharist. The Eucharist is the heart of the Church's life because Christ is the center of Catholic life. In Communion, Christ gives Himself totally, that we might share his life and be united in his mystical body.

In John 6:56 it says, "Whoever eats my flesh and drinks my blood remains in me and I in him." St. Augustine wrote that unlike natural food, which when consumed is changed into our substance, the Bread of Life changes and transforms us into Christ, strengthens us to live a Christ-like life and carry our crosses.

In 1985 a woman was pinned beneath a crane in New York City. As millions watched, TV cameras showed a team of paramedics fighting to keep her alive until a larger crane could be brought in to rescue her. The paramedics gave her fluids, blood transfusions, and massive doses of painkillers.

Then the woman asked to receive Holy Communion. Millions watched as she received the body of Christ. It was a beautiful testimony of her desire to receive the Eucharist to strengthen her in her hour of need.

In No. 1370 of the Catechism of the Catholic Church it says, "In communion with and commemorating the Blessed Virgin Mary and all the saints, the Church offers the Eucharistic sacrifice. In the Eucharist the Church is as it were at the foot of the cross with Mary, united with the offering and intercession of Christ."

Need for Unity

When we receive the Eucharist worthily, we are united more closely with Christ and others. To counteract harmful effects of polarization in today's Church and world, unity is needed. In First Corinthians 10:16-17, it says, "The bread which we break, is it not participation in the body of Christ? Because there is one bread, we who are many are one body for we all partake of the one bread."

May Eucharistic Adoration increase our desire to receive Christ in Communion. May the Eucharist unite us with Christ and others.

May it strengthen us in our journey through time to the fullness of eternal life in Heaven. In John 6:54 it says, "Whoever eats my flesh and drinks my blood has eternal life, and I will raise him on the last day."

3: Founder of Knights of Columbus Led Christ-Like Life

The 2012 Knights of Columbus State Convention will be held at Marriott West Hotel and Convention Center in Middleton on Saturday and Sunday, April 28 and 29.

Because of its nearness, as a Knight I thought that now might be a graced time to reflect upon the Christ-like life of the Venerable Fr. Michael Joseph McGivney, who founded the Knights of Columbus.

Humble Beginnings

He was born on August 12, 1852, in Waterbury, Conn. His parents were Patrick and Mary Lynch McGivney, Irish immigrants. His father worked as a molder in the heat and fumes of a brass mill.

Mary McGivney gave birth to 13 children. Six died in infancy. The McGivney children knew suffering and poverty. But they also enjoyed the blessing of growing up in a devout Catholic family where they learned lessons of faith, hope, and charity. These experiences influenced Father McGivney.

At age 13, Michael left school to work. At age 16, he left work to study for the seminary. In 1873 his father died. He left the seminary to help support his fatherless family.

Eventually, the bishop of Hartford enrolled him in St. Mary's Seminary in Baltimore. He was ordained on December 22, 1877, by Archbishop (later Cardinal) James Gibbons. He was quickly assigned to St. Mary Parish in New Haven.

The Knights Are Founded

In February of 1882, Father McGivney was acclaimed as founder of the Knights of Columbus by 24 men in St. Mary Church's basement. They recognized that without his optimism, will to succeed, and counsel, they would have failed. On March 29, 1882, the Connecticut legislature granted a charter to the Knights of Columbus, establishing it as a legal corporation.

Father McGivney founded the Knights to help meet certain problems. Sometimes virulent anti-Catholicism existed in the area, especially towards manual laborers. Too many young fathers died because of accidents or illnesses. The Knights sought to strengthen the faith of Catholic men, unite them to serve Church and community, and provide for financial needs when the breadwinner died or became incapacitated.

The Knights hoped to help members feel they were American citizens who "belonged" and to provide an alternative to joining the Masons. They chose Christopher Columbus as patron.

Largest Fraternal Organization

On August 14, 1890, Father McGivney died of pneumonia at age 38. His inspiration, leadership, and administrative drive earned him the affection of thousands.

Father McGivney established a Catholic fraternal benefit society that grew from humble beginnings to the world's largest Catholic fraternal organization with 1.8 million members and 15,000 councils. There are over 200 college councils and 5,000 circles of Columbian Squires, the Knights' official fraternity for boys 10 to 18.

The Squire Roses are a sorority for Catholic girls between ages 10 and 18, run by individual State Councils within the Knights of Columbus. The Daughters of Isabella, founded in 1897, as an auxiliary to Knights of Columbus, are composed of over 75,000 women in America and Canada.

In 2010 the Knights gave over $154 million directly to charity, donated over 70 million man-hours of volunteer service, and gave over 413,000 pints of blood.

Father McGivney's Legacy

The principles of the Knights are unity, charity, fraternity, and patriotism. The Knights have the highest respect for the pope, bishops, priests, and their chaplains. They seek to strengthen family life, reach out to widows and children of deceased Knights, and support Church teachings. They defend the unborn and aged and work to increase awareness of every Catholic's vocation.

Recognizing his heroic virtue, on March 15, 2008, Pope Benedict XVI honored him with the title "Venerable Servant of God." The next step would be for the Church to officially declare him "Blessed." This would require a miracle with clear evidence that the person(s) involved prayed to him for help.

For Father McGivney to be declared a saint, another miracle would be needed. Should this happen, he would be the first American-born priest to be canonized.

Chapter Two: Father's Day

1: Happy Father's Day to All Dads

Adam Hamilton tells a story about a camping trip he took with his two young daughters. The trip coincided with his birthday.

He explained to his two daughters that each could have 20 dollars to spend during the three days they were camping there. The two girls were so excited that they practically dragged their dad to the gift shop just outside the camp.

Rebecca, his daughter, who often thought with her heart, spotted a Brewers baseball cap. She immediately picked it up and tried it on.

"What do you think, Dad?" she asked.

Her dad, who was a Cubs fan, replied sternly, "You look pretty in it, Honey, but that hat costs 20 dollars! If you buy it, you won't have money left to spend the next two and a half days!"

"But Dad," Rebecca protested, "All I want is this hat and I really don't have any more money to spend!"

That evening they sat by the lake and watched the sun set like a beautiful orange red host into the chalice of the lake.

Rebecca hugged her dad and said, "Here is my birthday gift to you!" Then she put the hat on his head. "Happy birthday, Dad. I love you!"

Dad took Rebecca in his arms and hugged her. His tears mingled with Rebecca's tears.

The cap quickly became one of his most treasured possessions. He is now a Brewers fan. Every time he wears it, he thinks of Rebecca's sacrificial love for him. Rebecca reminds me of the widow who gave everything she had to the temple treasury.

Celebrating Fathers

We celebrate Father's Day on June 17 this year. Father's Day was started by Sonora Smart Dodd, who loved her father, William Smart, a Civil War veteran just as much as Rebecca loved her dad. With Dodd's help, he heroically raised six children after his young wife died while giving birth to their youngest child.

In 1909, while listening to a sermon about the newly recognized

Mother's Day, Dodd was bothered that there was not a day to honor fathers. So, she organized the first Father's Day in Spokane, Wash., on June 19, 1910.

On January 28, 2015, in his general audience catechesis, Pope Francis said, "Fathers play an irreplaceable role in family life, and their absence leaves children prey to false idols."

A father needs to spend quality time with his children.

One of the best gifts a father can give to his children is to love their mother. As Pope John Paul II said, "Children are the hope of the future!"

2: Compassionate and Good Examples

After Bubba Watson won the 2014 Masters, his two-year-old adopted son, Caleb, waddled onto the green to be embraced by his father. He reminded me of John F. Kennedy Jr., saluting his father's casket. Bubba Watson's wife followed Caleb, and the entire family basked in the moment of glory.

Bubba Watson's dad nicknamed him "Bubba" after former NFL player Bubba Smith, who was a good role model.

He said that his son Caleb is teaching him how precious life is. "He puts life in perspective," he said. "Golf is a game. When I play bad, he doesn't care. When I play great, he doesn't care. All he cares about is, 'Daddy give me a hug. Daddy pick me up.'"

Besides his family, another influence on Watson's game is his faith. "Looking at my son, I want to be as Christ-like as possible," Watson said. "I'll never be perfect. I'm always going to mess up, but my whole goal is to be the role model for my son." He isn't a role model just for his son, but to others. He thinks the President of the United States, others in authority, and all adults should be role models for the young.

Father's Day Origination

Fathers have a grave responsibility to give a good example to their children.

During the Great Depression, Jim Braddock was a washed-up penniless boxer, recovering from an injured hand. When a heavyweight contender's opponent was injured, with little or no training, Jim Braddock agreed to be the heavyweight contender's opponent.

He had no chance of winning and would probably last a round or so as a punching bag, but he desperately needed money to help feed his family.

Before the fight at supper his daughter cried from hunger pains. Moved with fatherly compassion, he gave his meager supper to his daughter and went into the fight hungry. What an inspiring act of sacrificial father love! Miraculously he won and eventually he became heavyweight champion.

Leave a Mark of Love

Caring fathers leave eternal marks of love on their children. The faith crisis of many young people today is often related to early life experiences when a good and loving father was missing.

The gentleness of my dad and Father Goetzman, my boyhood pastor, helped me to see God as a loving father and friend. My two brothers, three sisters, and I all loved Dad. He nurtured us, protected us, and shared Christian values. The way fathers relate to their daughter or daughters often influences how they relate to other men. A good father is also important to boys as a male role model.

Dad spent quality time with my brothers and me. He took us to baseball games. We hunted and fished together. He taught us to see nature as a window to God.

When Dad let me shoot his shotgun for the first time, it seemed like a rite of passage. He rescued me when my car broke down. He listened more than he talked, observed my mistakes, and gently corrected me. He even taught me to box to defend myself. He endured the teenage years of my siblings and myself. We gave him grey hair.

When I was in seventh grade, my parents bought a $1,000 house. They planned to move it from the country into town. After the first day, the movers left the house on a hill. To protect the house from strong winds, Dad and I stayed in it that night. If strong winds occurred, I didn't know what we'd do. But Dad knew and I felt brave and close to him.

Protector at All Costs

Dad hurt his back laying 12-inch cement blocks when I was in sixth grade. He seemed as helpless as Superman weakened by kryptonite, but he kept working in pain to support our family. I temporarily took his job shoveling coal in the church furnace. We rejoiced when a chiropractor cured his sciatica.

When I was in the Navy, I considered joining a Franciscan religious order which helped the poor. My dad sent me a prayer book. I gave it to the religious order and told Dad. He didn't like that. I think he thought that I should use if myself. He was right.

Arguably the best gifts that a mother can give to her children is to love their father. Mom occasionally criticized Dad, but when he came home from work, she treated him like a king. This communicated to us children that he was special. We agreed. Mom and Dad were partners in raising us children. They complemented each other. St. Joseph, Jesus' foster father, is the patron saint of fathers. He showed his love for Jesus by loving his mother. We can do the same.

Teaching Children About Jesus

Last Fall, Anglican Archbishop Justin Welby baptized Prince George. He told his parents that they have the task of teaching their son about Jesus. They should tell him about Jesus, read him stories about Jesus, and introduce him to prayer.

He said that unless three-month-old Prince George is united to Christ, he can do nothing. He told them that they must help George grow into the person God created and called him to be.

Pope John XXIII said, "It's easier for a father to have children than for children to have a real father." A father heard his son pray, "Dear God, make me the kind of man Daddy is." Later that night, the father prayed, "Dear God, make me the kind of dad my son wants me to be." Surely all dads can pray this prayer.

Let's pray that fathers are faithful to their challenging role. Wherever he is, let's wish him a happy Father's Day!

3: Pope Francis Praises Fatherhood

On February 4, 2015, at Vatican City, Pope Francis stated, 'Every family needs a father who shares in his family's joy and pain, hands down wisdom to his children and offers them firm guidance and love. Being a father is not easy. It takes lots of patience and grace."

Father Anthony Kadavil wrote, "Children who are raised with fathers present in the family have much lower rates of delinquency, drug and alcohol use, and teen pregnancy than those with absent fathers. The father's presence is also a significant positive factor in the children's getting a college education, finding a satisfying job, and making a lasting marriage. A girl's choice of partner and satisfaction in marriage is often directly related to the relationship she has had with her father."

Fathers (and mothers) teach us to pray, model values, and help to put the hope of Heaven in our heart. My Dad never missed Sunday mass and joined in praying the family Rosary. He respected priests and Sisters. His gentle kindness helped me to see God as my gentle loving Father.

At his general audience January 28, 2015, Pope Francis recalled how when he served as archbishop of Buenos Aires, he often asked fathers if they played with their kids, if they had the courage to love to "waste" their time with their children. The majority said, "Well, I can't, too much work."

In his book *Real Family Values*, Robert Lewis tells the heartwarming discovery workers at the Baseball Hall of Fame in Cooperstown, New York, made in 1993. While renovating the museum, they found a photo hidden in a crevice underneath a display case. The man in the picture had a baseball wooden bat resting on his shoulder. He wore a uniform with the word Sinclair printed across his chest. His expression was friendly and inviting.

Stapled to the picture was a note scribbled by an adoring fan. The note read, "You are never too tired to play baseball. On your days off, you helped build the Little League field. You always came to watch me play. You were a Hall of Fame dad. I wish I could share this moment with you. Your son, Peter."

Dr. Charlie Shedd once held a pop quiz contest called, "One Neat Dad." He asked contestants to recommend their dad for this great honor. The number one value that young people listed when they recommended their Dad for this contest was that "He takes time for me." Other qualities were, "He listens to me, plays with me, and invites me to go places with him. He lets me help him, treats my mother well (a biggie), and lets me say what I think. He is nice to my friends, only punishes me when I deserve it, and is not afraid to admit that he is wrong!"

Fr. Kadavil also stated that during the final year of her high school studies, St. Teresa of Avila was sent by her father (against her will) to a boarding house conducted by nuns. Her father took action at the moment he discovered bad books and yellow magazines hidden in her box. These had been supplied to Teresa by her spoiled friend and classmate, Beatrice. As Mother Superior, St. Teresa later wrote, "But for that daring and timely action of my father, I would have ended up in the streets, as a notorious woman."

St. Joseph is the patron saint of fathers. In the Jewish home, it was the Father who had the primary responsibility for his son's religious instruction. We believe that Jesus was the Son of God. He was the God-man. Still, in his human nature when the teenage Jesus went home and was subject to the influence of Joseph and Mary, he grew in wisdom, understanding and knowledge. Joseph, though barely mentioned in the Bible, was certainly an influential role model for Jesus in his human nature. Why else would Jesus have chosen the imagery of father to portray God and spend hours in prayer to his loving Father and seeking to do his will.

On Father's Day, like Sonora Dodd, we have a graced opportunity to thank our father. One of the best ways we can thank him is to be the best son or daughter that we can be. Whether he is yet alive or in eternity, may our dad enjoy a happy Father's Day.

4: Honoring Fathers for Their Special Love, Qualities

Mrs. Sonora Louise Smart Dodd was generally credited with organizing the first modern Father's Day. It was celebrated on June 19, 1910, in Spokane, Wash. The idea of Father's Day originated in Sonora's mind as she listened to a Mother's Day sermon in 1909.

Sonora's mother died while giving birth when Sonora was 16. William Jackson Smart, a Civil War veteran, raised the newborn and five other children with caring love. Sonora, the eldest child, admired the endless sacrifices her dad made so his children could live better. Consequently, she wanted a Father's Day to honor her father and other fathers. We celebrate Father's Day this year on June 20.

Gifts Fathers Share

Like Sonora, on Father's Day, we honor our father for the gifts he shared. Responsible fathers nurture, protect us, and share their values. A good father is important to boys as a male role model. The way that he relates to his son's mother can affect how his son or sons relate to women. How a father relates to his daughter or daughters helps to determine how she relates to other men. Caring fathers leave eternal marks of love on us.

Like Sonora Dodd, my three sisters loved their dad. I fondly remember how Donna, my little sister, waited for Dad to walk home from work. When she saw him, she ran out to meet him and leaped into his arms. "Daddy, I love you!"she cried. Unlike commercials, this was not staged. She proudly showed Dad her love and gave him "home."

Quality Time

My two brothers and I treasure the quality time that our father shared with us. Dad taught us to respect God's creation. Together, we hunted, fished, and watched ball games, prayed, worshipped, and enjoyed each other's presence.

Dad's gentleness helped us to see God as a gentle loving father. He never missed Sunday Mass and joined in praying the family Rosary. He respected priests and nuns. He joyfully brought our school's nuns a freezer. He did not limit his love to our family but shared it with others.

Loving Children's Mom

The best gift that a father can give to his children is to love their mother as Joseph loved Mary. When Dad retired, he got a job "running parts." It was delightful to see him stop for morning coffee at home (Ma's Café) because he wanted to enjoy her presence. He loved Mom.

Dad had many interests. He played cribbage and euchre. He and Will, his brother, were arguably the two most loyal local baseball fans in Kieler. He was a good storyteller and he liked people, especially children.

I watched him skillfully straighten dents out of car fenders at my uncle's garage. I enjoyed his humor and windy stories. Dad helped to keep my old klunker cars on the road. He became my favorite and cheapest mechanic.

St. Joseph is the patron saint of fathers. He was not Jesus' biological father but his foster-father. He showed his love for Jesus by loving Mary. He demonstrated that fatherhood involves more than biology. He was the model, guide, and teacher of Jesus. He supported the Holy Family by the work of his hands.

Good Father Qualities

In the *Norfolk Parenting Examiner*, Tanya Tringali lists the top ten qualities of a good father.
- They stick around. (Loyalty).
- They respect the women in their lives.
- They listen.
- They like to have fun.
- They show compassion. (Children need to see the softer side of fathers).
- They can be tough, yet fair.
- They have a good work ethic.
- They aren't afraid to own up to their mistakes.
- They have integrity. (They model values).
- They make their children feel protected.

A dad was about to tuck his five-year-old son into bed. The son prayed his usual prayer, "now I lay me down to sleep …". Then he looked up at his dad and prayed, "Dear God, make me a great big good man like my dad! Amen."

He fell quickly asleep. Then his father knelt and prayed, "Father, make me a great big good man like my son thinks I am. Amen." Inspired by St. Joseph, fathers can pray for the grace of being a good father.

The day after we buried Dad, I sat in the living room grieving silently. The door opened and I expected Dad to walk in as usual. Instead, Mom walked in and whispered, "Your dad was proud of you." Her words left an indelible mark of joy on my heart.

On Father's Day and each day, let us thank God for the gift of our father whose caring presence often mirrors or mirrored the love of our heavenly Father. Thank you, Dad, for helping to give me life and nurturing it. I am proud of you, too. "Happy Father's Day!"

5: Good Fathers Leave Eternal Marks of Love

Origin of Father's Day: Mrs. Sonora Louise Smart Dodd is generally credited with organizing the first modern Father's Day. It was celebrated on June 19, 1910, in Spokane, Wash.

When Sonora was 16, her mother died while giving birth. William Jackson Smart, a Civil War veteran, raised their newborn and five other children with fatherly love.

Sonora, the eldest child, admired the endless sacrifices her dad made so his children could live better. Consequently, she worked for a Father's Day to honor her father and other fathers.

Pope John XXIII said, "It is easier for a father to have children than for children to have a real father." Responsible fathers nurture, protect us, and share their values. They leave eternal marks of love on both sons and daughters. The way that a father relates to his children's mother can affect how his son or sons relate to other women.

Gentle Role Model

My little sister was born when I was five. I wanted my parents to name her Donald Arthur – Donald after me and Arthur after dad. They compromised by naming her Donna.

Donna loved dad. As a little girl, she ran out to meet him when he walked home from work. This was not a rehearsed commercial, but real love.

A good father is important as a male role model. I remember sitting on the splintered swing seats of Immaculate Conceptions School in Kieler with second grade classmates. We tried to out brag each other as to who had the best dad. "My dad can fix anything," one of us boasted. Another countered, "My dad is tougher than Joe Louis, the heavyweight boxing champion."

Dad taught my two brothers and me much by sharing quality time. Together we hunted, fished, watched ball games, prayed, worshipped, and enjoyed each other's presence. Passing on a hobby, a tradition, or skill to children is a priceless gift.

As father of our family, dad corrected me what I did wrong but in a gentle caring way. I listened and sometimes I repented and changed. Some educators call these teachable moments. His gentleness helped me relate to God as Heavenly Father.

Father and Son Communion

This year we celebrate Father's Day on the same day we celebrate the Feast of the Holy Trinity. In No. 2205 of the Catechism of the Catholic Church it says, "The Christian family is a communion of persons, a sign and image of the communion of the Father and the

Son and the Holy Spirit. In the procreation and education of children it reflects the Father's work of creation."

In No. 2214 of the Catechism of the Catholic Church it says, "The divine fatherhood is the source of human fatherhood; this is the foundation of the honor owed to parents. The respect of children, whether minors or adults, for their father and mother is nourished by the natural affection born of the bond uniting them. It is required by God's (fourth) commandment." The Catechism of the Catholic Church calls the family the domestic church and the original cell of family life.

St. Joseph is the patron saint of fathers. He was the model, guide, and teacher of Jesus, and he supported the Holy Family through the work of his hands. He shows us that the best gift that a father can give to his children is to love their mother as he loved Mary. Mary's love of Joseph surely influenced the profound respect Jesus had for women.

Being Just Like Dad

When Cal Ripken, Jr. was inducted into the Baltimore Orioles Baseball Hall of Fame, he told this story. His three-year-old son was engaged in a heated argument with his six-year-old daughter, Rachel. Rachel taunted Ryan, "You are just trying to be like your daddy."

Ryan thought for a moment and then countered, "What's wrong with trying to be like dad?"

After sharing this story, Cal Ripken, Jr., looked at his dad and exclaimed, "That is what I have always tried to do, to be a good person and a good father like my dad."

Like Sonora Dodd, we have a graced opportunity to appreciate our dad on Father's Day and every day.

If he is alive, we can visit him, share lunch, or call him. Perhaps the best way to honor him is to be the best son or daughter that we can be.

Whether he is in time or eternity, may our father enjoy a happy Father's Day.

Chapter Three: Independence Day

1: We Are A Nation of Immigrants

Independence Day on July 4 is a federal holiday when we celebrate the anniversary of the day when the Continental Congress adopted the Declaration of Independence.

Four days after the signing, the Liberty Bell rang to summon the people to the first public reading of the document. As the words were read, there were great shouts of affirmation and celebration.

A Nation of Immigrants

On Independence Day, we can recall that before and after the signing of the Declaration of Independence, America—with the exception of American Indians—was a nation of immigrants. Often immigrants came in search of a better life.

As a boy, history was my favorite subject. I knew my paternal grandfather came from Germany, but America was my home. I was proud to be an American and was grateful to men and women who made sacrifices and took a leap of faith to emigrate to an unknown country. Many immigrants came to America to escape persecution and to have freedom to worship according to their conscience. Many recent immigrants to America from what are now commonly referred to as the "less developed" countries have no problem in recalling vividly the sting of overt and unrelenting persecution and the blessings of our country.

Emma Lazarus wrote a sonnet entitled the "New Colossus" associated with the Statue of Liberty. Its most famous phrase was, "Give me your tired, your poor, your huddled masses yearning to breathe free." She saw the Statue of Liberty as a light of welcome for immigrants.

On Independence Day, our nation proclaims its dedication to liberty, justice, and equal rights and opportunities. Since we are blessed, we cannot turn within ourselves and ignore the needs of others.

Dependence Upon God

The signers of the declaration bravely pledged: "For the support of this declaration, with firm reliance on the protection of the Divine

Providence, we mutually pledge to each other, our lives, our fortunes, and our sacred honor."

Dependence upon God by the declaration's signers is clearly stated in the Declaration of independence, "We hold these truths to be self-evident, that all men are created equal, and that they are endowed by their Creator with certain unalienable rights." And it ends, "With a firm reliance on Divine Providence we pledge our lives, our fortunes, and our honor."

Recommitting Ourselves

We thank God for the abundant blessings given to our country. By the providence of natural resources coupled with contributions by many and diverse peoples who emigrated to these shores, we have become a great nation.

Recent popes reminded us that our greatness must be shown through our care for the most vulnerable. We must seek to include everyone in our blessings of prosperity.

On Independence Day, let us recommit ourselves to living the self-evident truths expressed in the Declaration of Independence. As Pope Francis urges, let us especially defend the rights of the unborn and others who are victims of injustice.

Let us pray for our government, the homeless, and the unemployed. May the Holy Spirit gift us with wisdom and courage to respect the dignity and rights of humans in all stages of life.

2: Making America Truly Beautiful

One of America's greatest blessings is the Declaration of Independence. Its preamble reads, "We hold these truths to be self-evident, that all men are created equal, that they are endowed by their Creator with certain unalienable rights, that among those are life, liberty, and the pursuit of happiness."

By the Grace of God

The words "One nation under God" in the Pledge of Allegiance, reinforce the Declaration's statement that God is the source of our nation's independence and freedom. From a Catholic perspective, freedom does not mean that we are free to do as we please. Rather, freedom means we are free to do as we ought.

True freedom comes from our dependence upon God, who graces us to recognize and respect the inherent dignity and rights of human persons stated in the Declaration of Independence. Secular humanism and original sin influence some Americans to deny or to become indifferent to God's ways. In Brothers Karamazov, Ivan says, "If God is dead, everything is permitted." When Jesus is alive in us and we follow his teachings, he gives us the grace to promote peace and respect life across the board.

Good civil laws help us to do what we ought, but inner personal conversion is also needed. In paragraph 1896 of the Catechism of the Catholic Church it is stated, "Where sin has perverted the social climate, it is necessary to call for the conversion of hearts and appeal to the grace of God. There is no solution to the social question apart from the Gospel."

In the Catechism of the Catholic Church No. 1903, it is stated, "Authority is exercised legitimately only when it seeks the common good of the group concerned and if it employs morally licit means to attain it." Freedom and liberty must be combined with responsibility to the natural law, the rights of others, and God's will.

Promoting the Common Good

In the Fortnight for Freedom Novena we prayed, "We praise and bless you (God) for the gift of religious liberty, the foundation of human rights, justice, and the common good. Grant to our leaders the wisdom to protect and promote out liberties."

We Catholics have the right and obligation to use our freedom to urge elected representatives to enact just laws that support the exercise of virtue. These include efforts to protect life, promote peace, and work for the equal rights of all. In the Catechism of the Catholic Church No. 1913, it says, "It is necessary that all participate, each according to his position and role, in promoting the common good. This obligation is inherent in the dignity of the human person." America must be careful not to impose its will and the American way on others by military might. This can send the message that justice comes about by force. Rather America should seek to respond to problems in peaceful ways at home and abroad.

In Living the Gospel of Life: A Challenge to American Catholics, the American bishops stated, "We encourage all citizens, particularly Catholics, to embrace their citizenship, not merely as a duty and privilege, but as an opportunity meaningfully to participate in building the culture of life. We urge our fellow citizens to see beyond party politics, to analyze campaign rhetoric critically, and to choose their political leaders according to principle, not party affiliation."

Living the Self-Evident Truths

On Independence Day, we can recommit ourselves to living the self-evident truths expressed in the Declaration of Independence, especially the rights of the unborn and others who cry for the right to live.

We can also pray for ourselves, our government, and other Americans during these difficult financial times. The Spirit will show us other ways to live the ideals of the Declaration of Independence if we ask.

May the Holy Spirit gift us with wisdom and courage so we can help make America more beautiful in the eyes of God and the world.

3: July 4th Invites Us To Reflect On Freedom

Independence Day is an American federal holiday commemorating the adoption of the Declaration of Independence on July 4, 1776. Studying the Declaration of Independence can motivate us to reflect upon the meaning of freedom and independence.

Dependence on God

We Catholics believe that our independence and freedom are rooted in our dependence upon God. Our dependence upon God is clearly stated in the preamble of the Declaration of Independence.

It begins, "We hold these truths to be self-evident, that all men are created equal, and that they are endowed by their Creator with certain unalienable rights, that among these are life, liberty, and the pursuit of happiness." The preamble ends with these courageous words, "With a firm reliance on Divine Providence we pledge our lives, our fortunes, and our honor!"

According to Denver Archbishop Samuel J. Aquila, for Christians, freedom is being free to choose Jesus Christ and follow his ways. It is also being free to choose the good for its own sake. When we fail to choose the good, we become slaves of evil or sin. Such slavery robs us of our freedom.

Freedom to Practice Religion

Venerable Fr. Samuel Mazzuchelli, who became an American citizen, believed that the Constitution guarantees citizens not freedom from religion, but freedom to choose and practice the religion they choose.

Those who push for freedom from religion today are often pushing their own religion of secular humanism. In the United States Catholic Catechism for Adults, it says, "In many ways attitudes and actions in the United States are in disbelief."

The first amendment, which prohibits the establishment of a state religion, has been interpreted so that it excessively marginalizes religion so that people of faith are pressured to act publicly as though religion doesn't matter. This has caused many believers to think that their faith is strictly society and politics.

Serving the Common Good

On September 16, 2013, in a homily at Santa Marta, Pope Francis stated, "Sometimes we hear that good Catholics are not interested in politics. This is not true: good Catholics immerse themselves in politics by offering the best of themselves so that the leader can govern. According to the Church's social doctrine, politics is one of the highest forms of charity, because it serves the common good. Catholics should offer their suggestions and prayers so their leaders can serve the common good in humility and love."

Public officials hold tremendous influence over public policies that affect us as citizens, Catholics, and people of faith. Issues of religious freedom, the right to life, protection of marriage and the family, the education of children, and how the poor, the vulnerable, and immigrants are served confront elected officials. These are the issues that we, too, as Catholics, must seriously evaluate when deciding for whom to vote.

Let's especially respect the rights of the unborn and others who literally cry for the right to live. Let's also pray for ourselves, our government, and other Americans during these challenging times.

Let's thank God that we live in "the land of the free," where we can enjoy the freedom to follow our conscience to worship God as we choose and believe.

4: Independence Day Helps Us Appreciate Our Blessings

Independence Day offers us an opportunity to thank God for our country's blessings. Some visitors from poorer countries express amazement at the cornucopia of blessings that we Americans enjoy and sometimes take for granted.

We celebrate some of our blessings when we sing "America the Beautiful." The words "God, mend thine every flaw" from this song can also invite us as responsible Catholics and citizens to try to help make America even more beautiful,

Independence Day is a federal holiday when we celebrate the anniversary of the day that the Continental Congress adopted the Declaration of Independence on July 4, 1776. On this day we can also thank God for the brave men who risked their lives and fortunes to eventually sign this great document.

The Knights of Columbus help us to remember the creator as the source of our blessings when we recite the Pledge of Allegiance. They led the movement to include the word "under God" in the pledge, which was approved by President Dwight Eisenhower on June 14, 1954. Later the president thanked the Knights for their efforts.

Because America is Good

America's belief in our creator as the source of our equality, freedom, and pursuit of happiness was recognized by Alexis de Tocqueville, the French historian and statesman who visited the United States to try to discover the secret of its greatness.

In Democracy in America, published in two volumes in 1835 and 1840, he observed, "Not until I went into the churches of America and heard her pulpits flame with righteousness, did I understand the secret of her genius and power. America is great because America is good. If America ever ceases to be good, America will cease to be great."

When God is alive in our lives, God can empower us to act morally and charitably towards others. Sharing our blessings sends the message that Americans are good, charitable people who care for the most vulnerable of humanity.

According to No. 1889 of the Catechism of the Catholic Church,

"Charity is the greatest social commandment – that is love of God and neighbor. It respects others and their rights. It requires the practice of justice and it alone makes us capable of it."

Religious Freedom

America must be careful not to impose its will and the American way on others by military might. This can send the message that justice comes about by force. Freedom and liberty must be combined with responsibility to the natural law, the rights of others, and the will of God.

Some openly try to remove God from our society under the guise of separation of church and state. Secular humanism and original sin help to produce Americans who deny God and who seek to impose freedom from religion.

Our nation has roots steeped in the commitment to religious freedom – the freedom to seek and to find equality before God under the established government. The Catholic colony of Maryland and other colonies were founded partially because of the desire for religious freedom.

A visiting priest told me that one of the God-given blessings of America is that when we disagree on important issues, we dialogue, debate, and vote. In his country when people disagree, there is a greater temptation to resort to violence or go to war.

Personal Conversion also Needed

Good civil laws can help us to do what we ought, but an inner personal conversion is also needed. In paragraph 1896 of the Catechism of the Catholic Church it is stated, "where sin has perverted the social climate, it is necessary to call for the conversion of hearts and appeal to the grace of God. Charity urges just reforms."

Efforts to protect life, promote peace and other God-given rights are stronger when Catholics live the teachings of the Church. As Catholics we have the right to use our freedom to urge elected representatives to enact just laws that support the exercise of virtue.

Independence Day offers us the opportunity to appreciate the blessings of our country and work to make it better. We can become more responsible Catholic citizens who ask God to mend the flaws in our country and ourselves.

We can pray for our government and our fellow citizens during these difficult financial times. Or we can respond in some other way that the Spirit leads us. May the Holy Spirit fill us with wisdom and courage so we can help to make America more beautiful in the eyes of God, America, and the world.

Chapter Four: Assumption

1: Mary's Assumption Inspires Us to Imitate Her Discipleship

As we begin Lent Fr. Mark Link shared an inspiring story of a Catholic teenager who felt that her mother rejected her. She transferred her anger for her mother to Mary. The girl reluctantly went on a required Confirmation retreat. The director talked about Mary. As the girl listened, angry feelings towards her mother surfaced. She rejected everything good the speaker shared about Mary. After the talk, she went outside to walk off her anger. She wanted to cry but her tears froze. She felt bitter loneliness and rejection.

She wandered aimlessly until her curiosity attracted her to a small grotto-like building. She looked inside and discovered a large statue of Mary from whom she was trying to escape. She wanted to run, but she was drawn to the kneeler at Mary's feet. She fell on her knees, weeping in the folds of Mary's robes. When she stopped crying, she felt cleansed and renewed. Touched by Mary, she began to accept her as her spiritual mother.

Later, she received the Sacrament of Reconciliation and felt the desire to forgive and be reconciled with her mother. She joined millions of Catholics who venerate Mary and feel her love for them. Her devotion to Mary inspired her to become Jesus' faithful disciple.

Exalted as Queen of Heaven

On August 15, we celebrate Mary's Assumption into heaven. In No. 966 of the Catechism of the Catholic Church it says, "The Immaculate Virgin, preserved free from all stain of original sin, when the course of her earthly life was finished, was taken up body and soul into heavenly glory, and exalted by the Lord as Queen over all things, so that she might be the more fully conformed to her Son, the Lord of lords and conqueror of sin and death."

The Second Vatican Council placed its teaching about Mary within the Constitution of the Church. The council wanted to emphasize that Mary was the model of discipleship and of Church. God sent the angel Gabriel to ask Mary to be Jesus' mother. She responded, "Let it be done to me as you say."

Mary's Assumption is God's response to her faithful discipleship expressed in her openness to doing his will. By being faithful disciples like Mary, we pray that when our earthly life ends, we will live not just in others' memories, but forever in glory, Mary, Christ's first and greatest disciple, shows us that because she followed Jesus, she experienced sorrow's crosses. Herod tried to kill Jesus and the Holy Family fled to Egypt. Jesus was lost in the temple. In his public life, he was in constant danger of being killed. Finally, he was cruelly crucified. As Christ's disciples like Mary we, too, will suffer.

Mary also shows us that as Jesus' disciples we experience joy. In Luke 1:39-56, the Assumption Gospel, Mary learns that Elizabeth, her elderly cousin, is pregnant with John, the Baptist.

Mary visits and helps her. She shares God's gift of Jesus in her womb with Elizabeth and unborn John who joyfully praise God. Mary shows us that helping those in need brings joy. Then she proclaims the Magnificat and invites us to follow its challenging message.

Like Mary, as a reward for faithful discipleship, we hope to enjoy Heaven where we will join Mary, the angels, saints, and loved ones.

We cannot comprehend Heaven's eternal joy and love. In first Corinthians 2:9 it is written: "What eye has not seen, and ear has not heard, and what has not entered the human heart, what God has prepared for those who love him."

Let us pray. Amen. Alleluia!

2: Mary's Assumption Inspires Us By Her Example

On November 1, 1950, more than 500,000 joyful people packed St. Peter's Square to hear Pope Pius XII proclaim the dogma of the Assumption of Mary into Heaven.

In Munificentissimus Deus, Pope Pius XII proclaimed that "the Immaculate Mother of God, the ever-virgin Mary, having completed the course of her earthly life, was assumed body and soul into Heavenly glory."

In No. 59 of the Dogmatic Constitution Lumen Gentium, the Second Vatican Council affirmed this dogma of the Church.

God's Children in Need

Pope Pius XII proclaimed the dogma of the Assumption to counter the loss of reverence and respect for the God-given identity of every human being.

In the first half of the 20th century, millions of persons who imaged God died in wars. Millions more died from poverty and diseases that could have been prevented by more active Christ-like concern.

War continues today. And according to the United Nations World Food Program, there are more than 925 million undernourished people in today's world. One in seven people goes to bed hungry every night. Most are children. Hunger and malnutrition are the number one risk to health worldwide – greater than AIDS, malaria, and tuberculosis combined.

Obligation to the Poor

In the Magnificat, from the Gospel of the Assumption, Mary reminds us of our obligation to the poor, the hungry, and those whom society regards as the least of God's people.

Early in his pontificate, Pope John Paul II visited Latin America, including all the then military dictatorships. In at least one country, government officials removed the Magnificat from his speech because of following words: "God has shown the strength of his arm and has scattered the proud in their conceit. He has cast down the mighty from their thrones and has lifted up the lowly. He has filled the hungry with good things and the rich he has sent away empty." Mary's Assumption reminds us that our bodies are temples of the Holy Spirit, destined for resurrection. She teaches us to respect our bodies and life across the board from womb to tomb. Mary, mother of the Prince of Peace, motivates us to work for peace in our families and in the world.

In the Magnificat, Mary also says, "From this day all generations will call me blessed. The Almighty has done great things for me, and holy is his Name."

We Catholics have helped to fulfill Mary's prophecy by calling her the Blessed Mother. In the "Hail Mary," we pray, "Blessed are you among women. And blessed is the fruit of your womb, Jesus."

Faithful Discipleship

Mary reminds us of our need to pray. As Mother of the Church, Mary devoted herself to prayer for nine days with the apostles in preparation for Pentecost when the Church was born.

From Mary, we can learn to listen, reflect, and live the Word of God. We can pray for the grace to be faithful to our baptismal promises and join Mary in Heaven.

Mary's Assumption is God's response to her committed discipleship. She is Christ's first and greatest disciple, who followed him to the cross when nearly everyone else abandoned him. Like Mary under the cross, being a faithful disciple can be lonely and difficult.

Paul Claudel, a great French Catholic writer, once wrote that the feast of the Assumption is for days when the rent is due, when the baby keeps crying, and it is raining outside (and inside). In such difficult times, we can seek Mary's help and intercession and imitate her faithfulness and openness to God's will.

Imitating Jesus

The Second Vatican Council placed the teaching about Mary within its document on the Church. This showed that Mary was the model for the Church and for every disciple. If we want to follow Mary into Heaven, we must strive to be a saint by imitating Jesus as she did.

On August 22, we celebrate the Queenship of Mary, the fifth glorious mystery of the Rosary. It follows the (glorious) mystery of her Assumption observed on August 15. Mary is queen, not because she wears a crown, but because of her response to grace. Her soul overflowed with the beauty of humility, obedience, and love.

In the Magnificat Mary says, "The Almighty has done great things for me." Mary adds, "God has mercy on those who fear him in every generation." We hope and pray for God's merciful judgment.

The Assumption of the Blessed Virgin speaks to our deep hope that we will live not just in the memory of others, but forever in glory. By imitating Mary's life of faithful discipleship through grace, we hope to enjoy God face to face in the Beatific Vision. With

Mary, the angels, and saints, we look forward to the joy of Heaven forever.

Chapter Five: Sports

1: St. Pope John Paul II – Future Patron Saint of Athletes?

Another season of high school, grade school, college, and professional sports has begun. These can invite us to reflect upon ways that we participate in sports as players or watch as spectators.

In Colossians 3:17, it says "Whatever we do in word or deed, do all in the name of our Lord Jesus Christ, giving thanks to God, the Father through him."

When Pope John Paul II became pope, he installed a swimming pool at Castel Gandolfo, his summer residence. He responded to those who criticized its cost by saying that it was cheaper than paying for a new conclave. He also skied. Doctors think that he recovered from an assassin's wounds quickly because of vibrant health nourished by sports. Through sports and exercise, he showed us ways to care for our bodies, which God created. If he is canonized, he could join St. Sebastian as patron saint of athletes.

On October 29, 2000, at Rome's Olympic Stadium, Pope John Paul II preached a homily entitled "Jubilee of Sports People." He stated, "Playing sports has become very important today, since it can encourage young people to develop important values such as loyalty, perseverance, friendship, sharing, and solidarity."

Respect for Teammates and Opponents

Church of God pastor Rev. John R. Wiuff seemed to agree when he encouraged athletes to model values. He wrote, "Athletes should treat teammates in encouraging and upbuilding ways, opponents with dignity and good sportsmanship, and game officials with great respect."

In the Journal of Lutheran Ethics, Dr. Robert Benne wrote, "It is impressive to see players help their fallen opponents off the floor or turf now and then, not only their teammates."

When I taught high school, I thought that our coaches modeled sportsmanship, discipline, and other values. Student athletes often impressed me by their commitment. I also respected non-athlete students.

The way we adults coach, play, or watch our favorite team is a visible way that our values connect with life. In sports, we keep score because one team must win (except in coach pitch and tee-ball.) We can show youth that winners are also those who do their best, play fairly, and learn lessons that help them cope with life.

Sports should be enjoyable and help youth grow as persons. I coached for 42 years and played baseball and softball for 12 years. It was hard, but fun. My winning percentage was slightly more than my weight.

Winning: The Ultimate Prize

A sports-minded lady told me she is proud when she sees her daughter play sports, but even prouder when she sees her in church. She believes like St. Paul that we should run the race of life for Heaven, the greatest prize!

Pope John Paul II ended his Jubilee 2000 homily on sports with this prayer, "Lord Jesus Christ, help these athletes to be your friends and witnesses to your love. Help them to put the same effort into personal asceticism that they do into sports; help them to achieve a harmonious and cohesive unity of body and soul.

"May they be sound models to imitate for all who admire them. Help them always to be athletes of the spirit, to win your inestimable prize: an imperishable crown that lasts forever. Amen."

2: Sports Offers Us Opportunities to Grow as Persons

After summer sports end, grade school, high school, college, and professional sports offer us fresh opportunities to reflect upon values that athletics helps to foster, especially in youth.

Recently on a sports talk show, the host lamented that there is much negative publicity about professional and sometimes college athletes regarding ways they give bad examples. He added that we don't hear enough about the good things such athletes do such as helping those in need and being good role models to youth in other ways.

Athletes as Good Role Models

I immediately thought of Gale Sayers, Chicago Bears Hall of Fame halfback, who tried to give good example to the young.

Roberto Clemente, Pittsburg Pirates Hall of Fame outfielder, was another of many good role models. In 1973, he died in the crash of a cargo plane carrying relief supplies to earthquake victims in Managua.

Teaching the Young

As sports fans, we have opportunities to be good sports and give good example to others. The way we coach or watch our favorite team play is one of the most visible ways our faith connects with life.

We can teach the young that sports can be enjoyable and provide opportunities for lifelong friendships. Athletic competition, carried out with sportsmanship and fair play, can help to foster loyalty, respect, and cooperation. Much depends upon the coaches, players, parents, and fans' values.

In 1 Corinthians 9:24-26, St. Paul says, "Do you not know that the runners in the stadium all run in the race, but only one wins the prize? Run so as to win. Every athlete exercises discipline in every way. They do it to win a perishable crown, but we an imperishable one."

Pope John Paul II ended his Jubilee 2000 homily on sports with this prayer, "Lord Jesus Christ, help these athletes to be your friends and witnesses to your love. Help them to put the same effort into personal asceticism that they do into sports; help them to achieve a harmonious and cohesive unity of body and soul."

"May they be sound models to imitate for all who admire them. Help them always to be athletes of the spirit, to win your inestimable prize: an imperishable crown that lasts forever. Amen."

3: Receiving Encouragement is Like Hitting a Home Run

Danny, a little league baseball player, readied himself, confident he would get a hit that would win the game. It was the last inning and the bases were loaded. There were two outs and the count was three balls and two strikes. Danny's team was one run behind. The ballpark was as quiet as a wake. Danny desperately wanted to impress his tense mom and dad, former ball players, who prayed while nervous fans gripped their programs. The funeral silence was broken by a prophetic voice, "No kid should be under this much pressure!" Many parents nodded agreement.

Danny swung – and he missed. Ecstatic opposing players and fans chorused their victory chant, "We're number one! We're number one!"

Danny felt like Peter after he denied Christ and the rooster crowed, "Guilty! Guilty!" He felt he had let his parents and teammates down. Striking out when your parents are watching is painful. I know! He tried to hide; but, how could he hide in a fishbowl?

Tears flooded Danny's face with failure. He felt someone tap his shoulder. He whirled around, with clenched fists, ready to fight his accusers. It was his Mom and Dad!

"Danny," they affirmed him, "You did your best! We love you just as much as if you hit a home run. Maybe more! We believe that you can do better; but we've been too busy over nothing important to practice with you like our parents did for us. That will change." Thanks to their encouragement and help Danny became a faithful Catholic and an excellent high school and college baseball player.

Parents have unique opportunities to encourage their children by helping them discover their gifts, sharing quality time, giving them a good religious education and teaching them to be part of a warm welcoming church.

Enrico Caruso, the great Italian tenor, wanted to quit singing after his music teacher said his singing sounded worse than mine. His mother encouraged him to continue. She sacrificed and walked barefoot to pay for his lessons. When Caruso became famous, he carried his mother's portrait with him. He asked for her prayers before every performance. Her encouraging words lived in his heart and inspired him to become a great singer.

Pastor Martin G. Collins wrote that sometimes we get too busy to be concerned about others. As Catholics, we must make time to be concerned about the welfare, happiness, and spiritual growth of others. Encouragement lifts the spirits of discouraged persons and helps them persevere during difficulties.

We all need occasional encouragement. Before entering the seminary, I quit work a week early so I could donate a week to helping build my relative's house. At the week's end, he said, "I hear you're entering the seminary." I replied, "I am," and prepared to receive his encouragement.

He replied, "I'll tell you frankly. You won't make it. You're too quiet." His remarks weren't encouraging, but there was probably some truth in them. I have never been a walkie talkie; but I would have preferred a mustard seed of encouragement especially after a free week of work.

When I completed high school, I wanted to do hard physical work, so I worked in a foundry. I doubted that I could do college work; but gradually I developed a thirst for education and enrolled at Platteville University under the G.I. Bill. Though one of my first classes was a remedial English course, surprisingly the teacher encouraged me to major in English. His encouragement rocketed my life in new directions.

The apostles re-named St. Barnabas "son of encouragement" when he became a Christian. In Acts 4:36 Barnabas sold his farm and donated the money to help the early church pay their bills. Before his conversion, Saint Paul persecuted Christians. When he was converted, because of his past, some Christians rejected Paul. However, Barnabas affirmed Paul and encouraged the Jerusalem community to receive him as a disciple.

Occasionally I wonder why I and others don't encourage or affirm others more? Is it because we lack self-confidence or suffer from indifference, competition, jealousy or fear that praising someone involves putting our self down? Is it because we aren't using the gifts and fruits of the Holy Spirit? Is it because we need a more Christ-like attitude?

Like Barnabas, to follow Jesus, we need to encourage others, avoid being judgmental and gossiping so we can build bridges, not barriers. Receiving the sacraments of Eucharist and Reconciliation helps us get closer to Jesus. Reading Sacred Scripture and the Catechism of the Catholic Church helps us remain faithful to Christ and His teachings.

In 1 Thessalonians 5:11 it says, "Therefore encourage one another and build each other up, just as you are now doing." Inspired by the example of Danny's parents, Caruso's mother, St. Barnabas and Jesus, let us encourage others through our words and deeds. It is one of the best gifts we can give to some who sorely needs it.

4: Respect is a Beautiful Virtue

One of the most beautiful words in the English language is the word "respect." Respect comes from the ability to look deeply (with Jesus' eyes) into a person and see their inner worth. We humans are so precious to Jesus that he died on the cross to redeem us from sin and offer us eternal life.

A Bible scholar said that Christ was hard on sin, but he was compassionate towards repentant sinners. He revealed this when he encountered the woman who was caught in the act of adultery. Jesus' enemies used her to try to trap him. They had no respect for her. After the woman's accusers left, Jesus took her aside privately because he didn't wish to embarrass her publicly. Very respectfully he asked her, "Has no one condemned you?"

"No one sir," she replied. Jesus replied compassionately, "Then neither do I. You may go! But from now on, avoid this sin!"

Larry Doby, the first African American baseball player in the American League, played for the Cleveland Indians. Doby was reputed to be a good player and excellent hitter. The first time he came to bat, he swung at the first three pitches and missed each by a foot. Fans booed him loudly.

Doby walked back to the dugout, sat down and tried to hide, but he couldn't. He was in a fishbowl. Joe Gordon, an all-star hitter, who always hit this particular pitcher well batted next. Everyone knew that he could not only hit the ball, but he could belt it out of the park. To everyone's surprise, Gordon swung at the first three pitches and missed each by a foot. A huge silence fell over the crowd. Gordon walked back to the end of the bench, sat down by Larry Doby and put his head in his hands.

Even today people wonder whether Joe Gordon struck out on purpose. No one knows for certain except Joe Gordon; but we know this, Larry Doby never went on the baseball field without picking up the glove of his teammate and handing it to him. They developed a tremendous respect for each other.

Once in a while, someone will hold a door open for me. I appreciate this. I know I am capable of opening the door by myself; but, to me holding the door is a sign of respect.

A marriage expert predicted that in a marriage if one treated the other disrespectfully, the relationship often failed. To feel respected, one partner must know the other genuinely respects them. Insincerity and flattery don't work. When we devalue others, we start treating them like objects, not people.

Good listeners show respect. The good listener says that you are important enough that I put aside everything and focus upon you because I value what you say! When we aren't listened to, we may feel like a balloon that is deflated and now has little or no value.

Poet Maya Angelou wrote, "If we lose love and respect for one another, this is how we finally die." Her wise words invite us to reflect upon how much we respect God, creation and each other.

Chapter Six: Labor Day

1: We Can Love, Serve God Through Work

Doing God's work includes serving as a Communion minister, usher, lector, serving on parish council or other Church related activities. Labor Day also reminds us that our work can be holy.

At the end of Mass, we are commissioned to "Go in peace to love and to serve the Lord." One way that we can love and serve God is through our work.

Praise God Through Work

This is significant because we spend much time working and going to and from work. But this does not happen automatically. We must desire to praise God through our work.

As a newly ordained priest, I once preached that the work of the school secretary was holy. She thanked me and said that she never realized her work could be holy.

A mother said, "My marriage is a gift from God. Presently my vocation is mom and wife. With six growing children, I live most of my Christianity outside of church doors. My work includes changing diapers, making ends meet, cleaning, washing, planning, encouraging my family, and much more. My husband and I offer our work to God as prayer, and we try our best to help our children grow in faith. We believe that we are doing God's work and that our work is holy."

Sr. Grace Remington does the same in her vocation as a Cistercian nun. She and her community praise God through cooking, gardening, washing clothes, interactions with others, study, prayer, Mass, and in whatever they do.

A single girl praises God when she stacks supermarket shelves. She makes her work meaningful because she prays for those who will purchase the items she stacks.

Doing Our Best

In his encyclical, On Human Work, Pope John Paul II basically said that we make ourselves by the work that we do. Doing our best at work helps to build character. Feeling our work is worthwhile, receiving just compensation, and making our work a prayer helps us to do quality work.

Research indicates that our success at work often depends upon how well we work with and relate to coworkers. We reveal our Christianity when we treat others in a Christ-like way. I experienced this during appointments at my former dentist. He and his staff joked and treated me, other patients, and each other with humor respect and love. This helped them to work hard and well. It also helped patients to relax and feel better.

I especially remember the day when at noon my car had a flat tire. The dentist changed the tire for me. I felt good. I joked that I would surely receive a bill, but I never did. My present dentist has a similar spirit in his office.

In Holiness in the Workplace Elizabeth Dreyer states that the more workers love each other, the more creative they become in solving work problems. We help to bring God's peace and love to the workplace when we pray for, support, and offer encouraging words to fellow workers especially when they are hurting.

Co-Create with God

Whether we are a marketing person, carpenter, homemaker, baker, seamstress, teacher, dentist, or doctor, we co-create with God in our work. We contribute to God's continuing work of sustaining creation. Making a crutch from wood, bread from flour, or beautiful gowns from silk are examples of co-creation. We practice Co-conservation when we conserve raw materials. Farmers, waitresses, grocers, and cooks feed the hungry. Doctors and nurses minister to the sick as do mothers who make chicken noodle soup to cure family colds.

Members of the Retired Priest's Ministry help aged priests. From their just wages, Christian workers give to the poor, disabled, underfed, underprivileged, and others in the same fragile boat of need.

Management is also a sacred task because managers handle people's lives. Businesses should seek to make a profit, but the priority of persons over money is the more than 100-year-old Catholic principle that guides the Church's insights into work.

Honor Dignity of Workers

Labor Day is a national holiday when we honor the dignity of workers and the quality and importance of their work. Inspired by the example of Jesus and St. Joseph, on Labor Day we can pray that workers praise and thank God through their work and Christ-like relationships with others. We can also pray that those who are looking for work find jobs.

May we enjoy a holy, restful Labor Day that renews us to keep making our work holy.

2: Labor Day Invites Us to Reflect on Our Work

Labor Day has become a day of parades, picnics, and political speeches. Many see this day as a celebration of summer's end, the beginning of school, and one more chance to relax before fall's busyness. Labor Day did not begin with this intention.

On September 5, 1882, the first Labor Day celebration and parade in the United States was held in New York City. Thousands of workers marched in a parade up Broadway carrying banners that read: "EIGHT HOURS FOR WORK, EIGHT HOURS FOR REST, EIGHT HOURS FOR RECREATION." It became a federal holiday in 1894.

Reflecting on Dignity of Work

In 1891, in his ground-breaking encyclical Rerum Novarum, Pope Leo Xll outlined the rights of workers to a fair wage, safe working conditions, and formation of labor unions, while affirming the rights of property and free enterprise.

Labor Day offers us the opportunity to reflect upon the dignity of work, the necessity of work, and work's dangers.

The Book of Genesis tells us that originally work gave joy, satisfaction, and pleasure. After Adam and Eve's sin, work was seen as a curse. In Genesis 3:19, when God banished Adam and Eve from the Garden of Eden, God said, "In the sweat of your face shall you get bread to eat."

Work Can Be Redemptive

In No. 2427 of the Catechism of the Catholic Church it says, "Work honors the Creator's gifts and talents to us. Work can also be redemptive. By enduring the hardships of work in union with Jesus, the carpenter of Nazareth and the one crucified on Calvary, man collaborates in a certain fashion with the Son of God in his redemptive work. He shows himself to be a disciple of Christ by carrying his cross daily in the work he is called to accomplish."

In Towards a Catholic Work Ethic, Ed Marciniak wrote, "Honest work and excellent craftsmanship extend God's creative work." Workers who make crutches, crucifixes, or build houses transform raw materials that God created into products that benefit others. Workers who grow crops, wait on tables, work with a computer, or prepare meals benefit others.

Finding Joy in Our Work

We enjoy doing what we do well. Finding joy and satisfaction in our work is a gift. Doing our best at work helps to build character.

Judge Charles Corkery wrote an eloquent obituary about the Venerable Fr. Samuel Mazzuchelli that included him enjoying his work. He wrote, "There he is high up on the scaffold, sleeves tucked up, industriously at work in brick and mortar. In the evening he is in the pulpit discoursing on some abstruse question of Christian philosophy. Tomorrow he lectures before the governor, judges, and legislatures on the science of political economy, but always and everywhere present when the sacred duty of the ministry required. Wonderful little man!"

A mother said, "With six growing children, my work includes changing diapers, making ends meet, cleaning, washing, planning, encouraging my family, and much more. My husband and I offer our work to God, and we try our best to help our children grow in faith. We believe that our work is holy."

Reducing Joblessness

Today, millions are without work and millions more are underemployed, working at part-time jobs or jobs that do not pay a decent wage. Society has a moral obligation to reduce joblessness because it is through work that families are sustained, children are nurtured, and the future is secured.

On this Labor Day, let us ask St. Joseph, the patron saint of workers, to pray for us. Let us thank God for the talents and work he has given us to do and use them to help build God's kingdom on earth. Finally, let us pray that the jobless find work that sustains their family and secures their future.

3: Labor Day - Reflecting Upon Spirituality of Work

Labor Day invites workers to reflect upon their work's spiritual value. This is important because most active adults spend the majority of weekday hours awake, working, commuting to work, preparing for work, or resting from work. Many retired persons including priests, also work in various ways. I know! St. Benedict said, "To work is to pray." Brother Lawrence made his work in the kitchen a prayer that brought him closer to God. In Colossians 3:17, it says, "Whatever you do in word or work, do everything in the name of the Lord Jesus, giving thanks to God, the Father, through him."

Whatever Your Work, Do it Well

Since the early Church, Catholics have offered their work to God as a prayer. We Catholics can continue to offer our work to God at Mass, in our morning offering, while we work, and in other ways.

Dorothy Sayers wrote that it is unfortunate that on Sundays in the homily, a carpenter may hear, "Don't get drunk on Saturday and be sure to give generously to the collection." Instead she says that they should hear, "Be the best carpenter you can be." Whatever your work, do it well.

At a rare parish help-out, I noticed that a man who received Communion had paint imbedded in the cracks of his hands. They reminded me of dad's hands. After Mass I told him that his hands reminded me that like St. Joseph, he did an honest days' work. St. Joseph is the patron saint of workers.

A spirituality of work might mean doing the best we can at work, saying a quick prayer or praising a co-worker. It often includes the difficult task of respecting colleagues.

Opportunities to Do God's Work

Research indicates that success at work often depends upon how well we work with and relate to co-workers. We reveal our Christianity when we treat others in Christ-like ways. According to Stewardship: A Disciple's Response, a woman who works at a supermarket check-out counter stated, "I feel that my job consists of a lot more than ringing up orders, taking people's money, and bagging their groceries. By doing my job well, I know that I have the chance to do God's work, too. I try to make my customers feel special. While I serve them, they become the most important people in my life."

Workplace spirituality includes ensuring just wages and safe working conditions, giving a full day's work, utilizing grievance procedures, forgiving, communicating openly and respectfully, developing personal talents, and contributing to the common good.

A graced spirituality of work helps workers balance work with family, Church, and community obligations. Married persons especially should avoid the trap of gradually becoming married to their work rather than to their spouse. If this happens, when they are needed, husband and wife may not be there for their loved ones.

Understanding Others' Burdens

Because I was ordained at a later age, I enjoyed varied work experiences. I think this has helped me to better understand the work of others. I worked in construction for two years, four years in a Navy foundry, on farms, factories, and taught over two years in public schools before I entered the seminary. I also coached baseball for 42 years as priest and lay person.

As a priest, I served as parochial-vicar and pastor. I did minor maintenance work, mowed parish lawns, shoveled snow, checked doors and windows every night, and more. I served as full time teacher-chaplain at Beloit Catholic High for 20 years. As a high school sophomore, I worked on a farm and got pinned between a big Case tractor and a harrow. I promised God that if I were rescued, I would become a priest. The farmer rescued me. But I quickly forgot my promise. The farming accident was not why I became a priest. But I think that it was a step along the way.

An Honest Day's Work

I fondly remember the statue of St. Joseph in front of Beloit Catholic High and in St. Paul's Church in Beloit. His example of honest work in the carpenter shop can inspire us to bring meaning to our work. We can pray that his example gifts us with patience, perseverance, and hope as we work. We can ask the intercession of St. Joseph for the unemployed because he experienced unemployment. When Herod tried to kill Jesus, Joseph had to leave his thriving carpenter business in Nazareth and flee to Egypt with a minimum of possessions. There he had to begin again to find work and new customers.

Doing one's best at work helps to build character. Feeling work is worthwhile, receiving just compensation, and making work a prayer, helps workers to do quality work. Workers can also pray for employers and co-workers who bear heavy burdens.

Let us pray that Labor Day inspires workers to praise and thank God through their work and Christ-like relationships with co-workers, employers, and employees. May we, and all workers enjoy a sacred, restful Labor Day that helps us all enjoy each day of work as a grace!

4: Making Our Work a Prayer

In the 15th century in a village near Nuremberg, Germany, Albrecht Durer and his brother Albert dreamed of attending art school.

But Albrecht Sr., their father who supported 18 children, understandably couldn't afford to send them. So, the two brothers made an agreement. Albrecht would attend art school while Albert worked in the mines to pay his expenses. When Albrecht graduated, he would use his artistic talents to pay for Albert's tuition and other expenses.

Brother's Sacrifice

After four years, Albrecht Jr. finally graduated. His family and friends gathered to share a dinner of thanksgiving. Albrecht began the celebration by proposing a toast to his brother who sacrificed by paying his expenses for art school.

"Brother," he said with deep emotion, "Your sacrifices helped me to achieve my dream. Now it's my turn to help you follow your dream. I've already earned enough money from my drawings to pay the first year of your tuition at art school. You can enroll whenever you wish. I'll pay for all your expenses until you graduate."

With tears streaming down his face, Albert cried, "No, no, brother, it's too late! I cannot accept your generous offer. You see, the work in the mines was so hard that I broke every finger in my hands at least once! Then arthritis crippled my hands so badly that I can't even lift this glass to return your toast, let alone hold a pen or brush to do delicate artwork. So, brother, it is too late for me."

According to tradition, out of gratitude for his brother's sacrificial love, Albrecht painstakingly drew his brother's abused hands with palms together and thin fingers pointing skyward. He called this drawing Hands," but people renamed it "Praying Hands." It has become world famous.

Work Can Be a Prayer

This prayerful, inspiring drawing reminds us that we pray with our hands raised to Heaven as a sign of humility and dependence upon God. As I reflected upon "Praying Hands," I realized that we also pray with our hands in other ways.

In today's technological society, we still work with our hands, using the computer, kneading dough, and more. The work we do with our hands can be a prayer when we make it an offering of love to God and neighbor.

Albert's crippled hands remind me that when I was a boy, there were more men with missing fingers and hands than today. They remind me, too, that when I was a high school sophomore, on my first day on summer construction, I swung a sledgehammer all day and developed so many blood blisters that I couldn't hold a bat at baseball practice that evening.

Father's Paint-Stained Hands

"Praying Hands" also reminds me of my Dad's hands. His paint-stained hands were holy because Dad used them to provide for the family.

Once at a parish "help-out," I noticed that a man who received

Communion also had paint imbedded in the cracks of his hands. After Mass I told him that his hands reminded me of Dad's hands. I told him that, like St. Joseph, they showed that he did an honest days' work. (Of course, one can also do honest work with clean hands.)

Doing Quality Work

We can offer our work to God in prayer in the morning offering, by doing quality work, by helping others, and in other ways. Doing one's best at work helps to build character. Feeling work is worthwhile, receiving just compensation, and making work a prayer helps us to do quality work. We can also pray for our employers and co-workers. We can pray for the unemployed, help them find work or, if feasible, we can hire them for some work.

The Spirituality of Work

Labor Day is a national holiday when we honor workers' dignity and the quality of their work. It offers us opportunities to reflect upon the spirituality of our work.

Most active adults spend the majority of their waking hours during the week working, commuting to work, preparing for work, or resting from work. Others work in their homes. Many retired persons, including priests, also work in various ways.

Let's pray that Labor Day inspires us to praise and thank God through our work and Christ-like relationships with co-workers, employers, or employees. May we and all workers enjoy a renewing Labor Day that helps us to make each day of work a holy day and a prayer. Amen!

PART VII: FALL

Chapter One: Grandparents

1: Grandparents Day Connects Generations with Bonds of Love

In 1978 President Jimmy Carter proclaimed that National Grandparents Day would be observed on the first Sunday after Labor Day. This year we observe Grandparents Day on September 12. We remember and thank those who helped to make this special day possible.

We thankfully remember Hermine Beckett Hanna, for her contributions to Grandparents Day. On February 21, 1990, New York Congressman James T. Walsh officially recognized her efforts on behalf of grandparents

Also, we gratefully remember Michael Goldgar, who proposed Grandparents Day in the 1970s. After he visited his aunt in an Atlanta nursing home, he spent $11,000 of his own money in lobbying and meeting frequently with legislators to have Grandparents Day officially recognized.

Finally, we thank the Senate and former President Jimmy Carter who officially recognized Marian McQuade as the founder of National Grandparents Day. Mrs. McQuade encouraged grandchildren to tap the wisdom and heritage of their grandparents and suggested that the young adopt a grandparent.

The official song of National Grandparents Day is "A Song for Grandma and Grandpa" by Johnny Prill. The forget-me-not is Grandparents Day's official flower.

Honoring Our Grandparents

On Grandparents Day we recognize our parents and especially our grandparents for influencing our lives. Dr. Arthur Kornhaber, grandparent and founder of the Foundation for Grandparenting, states that one of the most significant gifts in a child's life is a loving bond with grandparents.

Unlike many busy, multi-tasking parents, grandparents have more time to create wholesome memories such as going for ice cream, telling stories, or recognizing the stars of the big dipper! My neighbors enjoy their grandchildren in these and other ways. Young and old take turns enriching each other.

Children valued by grandparents tend to do better in school and to feel comfortable with older people. The comfort that a grandparent can provide helps grandchildren feel safe, secure, and loved.

A grandmother I know passes on traditions to her grandchildren. She bakes a birthday cake and gives it to her grandson on Christmas Eve. Then they celebrate Jesus' birthday with Bethlehem joy.

If they are alive, we can remember grandparents by sharing a bouquet of forget me-not flowers, a card, a phone call, or lunch. We can also visit grandparents who are shut-ins or nursing home residents. If they have died, we can ask them to pray for us or we can pray for them.

Since Grandparents Day falls on a Sunday, some schools offer grandparent activities on school days. They invite grandparents to participate in special assembly programs or, if a Catholic school, a Mass. Sometimes students share story-telling activities or artwork that relate to their grandparents. At St. Joseph School in Sinsinawa, the school invited grandparents to a Mass and reception.

Fond Memories

Some say that when a baby is born, new grandparents are born. I fondly recall a nursing home resident named Sally whom I visited regularly. Her dream was to hold her baby granddaughter. She bubbled with joy as she told me how good she felt when she finally held her dream.

My paternal grandparents died before I was born. But I feel I know them somewhat through stories. Relatives say that I inherited some of their traits. Still, I wish I had known them.

When I was a boy, I waited eagerly for my other grandpa to come to town. I enjoyed visiting my grandparents' farm which was a circus of delights, surprises, and dangers. There I remember cutting my finger badly. I can still smell the liniment that Grandma put on the cut. Dad drove me to the doctor. The finger required stitches. Every time I smell liniment, I recall Grandma's healing care. Our richest memories are often steeped in smells, feelings, and flavors.

Recently I heard a young boy proudly tell his grandparents and me that Ryan Braun, his favorite baseball player, threw him a baseball at a Brewers game. This is the highlight of his young life,

On July 26, 2009, following the Angelus, Pope Benedict stated that the educational role of grandparents is important especially when parents are unable to dedicate an adequate amount of time to their children. The pope then asked the faithful to pray for grandparents "who in families are often witnesses of the fundamental values of life." Then he entrusted to the protection of St. Ann and St. Joachim, the patron saints of grandparents, all grandparents of the world.

The pope's remarks remind me of a grandmother who baby-sat her grandson. She often shared how she tried to influence him by teaching him prayers and Christian values. Occasionally I ask youngsters to share who reminds them of Jesus. Often, they reply with emotion, "Mom, Dad, Grandma, or Grandpa."

May the Father bless grandparents. May Jesus give grandparents peace and health. May the Holy Spirit inspire us to remember and appreciate our grandparents on Grandparents Day and every day.

2: Good Grandparents Add Meaning to Our Lives

Some say that grandparents have the benefits of grandchildren, but none of the responsibilities. I don't think this is always true. Marian McQuade, the founder of Grandparents Day, agrees with me. She noticed that when parents were absent or unable to raise their children, grandparents often stepped in and made a difference.

Many grandparents give their grandchildren a sense of security and help to keep families together. Sometimes they take a direct role in their grandchildren's lives due to family breakdowns and sometimes because of increases of single parenthood. A grandmother I know was torn between raising her grandson or adopting him out. Because of her age, raising her grandson would require heroic adjustments. I don't know what she decided.

Sometimes I ask children to name someone who reminds them of Jesus. Often, they say, "My grandma and my grandpa are kind, loving and generous like Jesus." The greatest gift grandparents can give to their children is to love them.

Bob unexpectedly experienced a grandfather's sacrificial love on his early morning walk. A garbage truck stopped. The driver showed

Bob a photo. He said, "This is my grandson. He is on life support." Assuming the driver was begging for money for the hospital bill, Bob reached for his wallet, but the driver told Bob that he wanted something more than money, "Could you please pray for my grandson," the driver pleaded tearfully.

Some grandchildren are curious about their grandparents. I know I am. My paternal grandparents died before I was born. I know them vicariously through stories that Dad and Mom shared. I did know my maternal grandparents. As a boy I eagerly looked forward to family gatherings at their farm. I avoided their mean roosters who scared me.

Grandparents are an open book of family history. My maternal great grandmother died when grandma was young. Since she was the oldest child, Grandma became the family's mother. Once when she and her sisters were alone, a stranger came by. Reluctantly she opened the door. With a German accent, the stranger asked, "Do you vant buy sum kindlin vood?" Grandma laughed at this funny man. A sister scolded her, "Don't laugh. Someday you may marry him." She did and I'm glad.

Most living grandparents appreciate hearing from their grandchildren. They both need each other's love! A letter, a telephone call or visit can make a grandparent's day, if needed, younger grandchildren could ask their parents to help them write a letter.

Whether they are living or deceased, let's give our grandparents a "Happy Grandparents' Day" by being the best grandchild we can be!

Chapter Two: Fall Saints

1: Autumn Reminds Us of St. Francis

We celebrate the feast of St. Francis of Assisi on October 4. This is appropriate because Francis loved God's creation.

During autumn, God creatively works through nature to convert fall's leaves to a beautiful scarlet and gold. This change reminds us that God changed Francis from a carefree green youth into a committed Christ-like saint. His conversion invites us to ask God to also change us.

Through the ages, Catholics, non-Catholics, and non-Christians have loved Francis. He has influenced millions by his pure Christ-like goodness, love of creation, and joy. Because Francis is my middle name, I consider him to be my patron saint.

The Early Life of Francis

Francis was born at Assisi in 1181 or 1182. Pietro Bernardone, his father, was a prosperous merchant. Francis planned to follow in his footsteps. He also dreamed of being a troubadour or knight who won fame and honor.

In 1201, he joined an attack on Perugia, a rival city. He was captured and imprisoned for a year. He became severely ill and turned to God, gradually.

Around 1205, he joined another military expedition to Apulia, another rival city. Hoping to win glory, he bought an expensive suit of armor decorated with gold. After a day's ride from Assisi, Francis dreamed that God told him to return home and serve him.

Once home, he was humiliated, ridiculed, and called a coward by villagers. His father scolded him for the money he wasted on armor.

A Slow Conversion

After this, Francis started to spend more time in prayer. Sometimes God's grace overwhelmed him with joy. His conversion was slow, yet steady.

Once Francis unexpectedly encountered a leper. Repelled by the leper's appearance and smell, Francis nevertheless kissed his hand. The leper returned his kiss, and Francis rejoiced. As he rode away, he turned to wave but the leper disappeared. Francis treasured this encounter as a test from God that he passed.

In 1206, while he prayed at the run-down church at San Damiano, he heard Christ on the crucifix speak, "Francis, repair my church." Francis assumed this meant the crumbling church where he knelt.

So, Francis sold fabric from his father's shop to get money to repair the church. His father considered this stealing. He dragged Francis before the bishop and demanded that he return the money and renounce all rights as heir.

The bishop advised Francis to return the money and trust that God would provide. He did. Then Francis abandoned all his rights and possessions, including his clothes. Wearing castoff rags, he left his father and went into the frigid woods, singing. After this, Francis who had nothing had everything.

Rebuilding the Church

After rebuilding San Damiano and two other churches, Francis realized that Christ wanted him to help rebuild the church as people, not buildings. Scandal, avarice, and heresies had weakened the Church. So, Francis began to preach. He emphasized simplicity and poverty, relying on God's providence rather than worldly goods. Companions soon joined him. He gave them a short rule which Pope Innocent III approved. He called them Friars Minor. They worked or begged for what they needed. Surplus was given to the poor.

Francis turned his troubadour skills to writing prayers and hymns for Christ. With Francis' encouragement, Saint Clare founded a sisterhood at San Damiano, called the Poor Ladies. Later they were named the Poor Clares.

Concern for all God's Creatures

The Church honors Francis as the patron saint of animals and ecology. Every year on the Sunday nearest his October 4 feast day, Catholic and other Christian churches around the world offer services where animals are blessed. These services celebrate God's concern for all creatures.

Francis believed that as God's creatures, it is our duty to protect and enjoy nature as stewards of God's creation. He is well known for writing the "Canticle of Brother Sun and Sister Moon." His respect of creation led him to the Creator. Saint Francis became a deacon, but he felt he was unworthy of the priesthood. He was strengthened by the Eucharist which he loved. Francis shows us that simplicity of life frees us to love, worship and serve God.

Francis sought to follow fully and literally the gospel way of life demonstrated by Christ. As Francis prayed to share in Christ's passion, he received in his own body the stigmata, the marks of the nails and the lance wound that Christ suffered.

Christ continues to rebuild his Church through the spirit of Christ embodied in St. Francis. In the prayer of St. Francis, we ask for Francis' Christ-like spirit when we pray that we might not so much seek to be consoled as to console, to be loved as to love, to be understood as to understand, for it is in giving that we receive.

It has been said that when Francis died, there was silence. Then the birds sang. Amen.

2: Saint Raphael – Patron Saint of Madison Diocese

On September 29, we honor three archangels. They are St. Michael, who is also known as the Warrior, St. Gabriel, who is called the Messenger, and St. Raphael who is known as the Companion.

The Venerable Fr. Samuel Mazzuchelli named three churches that he helped to build in the tri-state area after these three archangels. They are St. Gabriel of Prairie DuChien, Wisconsin, St. Raphael of Dubuque, Iowa, and St. Michael of Galena, Illinois.

The cathedrals of the Dubuque Archdiocese and Madison Diocese had the rare distinction of being named after St. Raphael the Archangel as patron saint. St. Raphael is one of three archangels mentioned by name in scripture and one of the seven who stand before God's throne.

Madison's Cathedral

In the early 1840's, Irish immigrants settled in what later became Madison. They were soon organized into a parish named after Michael the Archangel. On August 15, 1842, Mass was offered for the first time by Father Martin Kundig. The land that the parish buildings and the later parking lot would be built upon land was donated by Governor James Duane Doty who was a close friend of Fr. Samuel Mazzuhelli. From 1842 until 1853 the parish did not have a church of its own. Mass was often celebrated in homes and in the state Capitol building.

In 1853, Fr. Francis Etchmmann led the construction of the current church building that has been damaged by fire. The cornerstone was laid in 1864. Archbishop John Michael Henni of the Milwaukee Archdiocese dedicated the new building. In 1885, the new bells and spire were added.

On January 9, 1946, Pope Pius XII created the Diocese of Madison from an eleven-county area in southern and southwestern Wisconsin. Territory was taken from the Archdiocese of Milwaukee and from the Diocese of LaCrosse. (I remember when this happened). St. Raphael Parish was chosen as the cathedral parish for the new diocese. Msgr. William Mahoney was chosen as the proud pastor of St. Raphael, the patron saint of our diocese.

St. Raphael's Patronage

Recently, I was delighted to rediscover that St. Raphael, our Diocese's patron saint, is also the patron saint of many areas of concern that touch our lives. St. Raphael is the patron saint of sick persons, travelers, bearers of sick persons, bearers of the good news, happy meetings, the blind, physicians, nurses, and the choice of a god spouse. In addition, St. Raphael is the angel of good health, chaste relationships, health and happy marriages.

St. Raphael is also the defender of the church, strong helper in time of need, angel of home life, and guardian of the Christian family. Too, St. Raphael is the angel of joy, support of the dying, and healer of the sick.

According to the September 2, 2007, issue of the Catholic Herald, the St. Raphael's Pilgrim's Marriage Prayer Group has been formed in our diocese. Members of the Group commit themselves to daily prayers of sacrifice for marriage prep facilitators and engaged couples in our diocese.

Members are also asked to pray a novena to St. Raphael leading up to the weekend. The group has taken St. Raphael as their patron saint not only because he is the patron saint of the Madison Diocese, but also because of his role in Sarah and Tobias's marriage.

Providentially, it seems the Holy Spirit has helped our diocese to wisely choose St. Raphael as its patron saint. Tragically, St. Raphael's church was destroyed by a fire in 2005. The construction of a new cathedral is on hold. Holy week services and other important events involving the Bishop are often held at St. Maria Goretti, Queen of Peace church in Madison and the Catholic Center.

As our diocese prepares to rebuild the cathedral and move into the future, let us learn from St. Raphael and ask the archangel's intercession for healing, safe travel, support of the ill, the dying, family and other concerns.

Though St. Raphael does not now have a home church in our diocese, from Heaven the archangel guides and intercedes for us.

St. Raphael also lives in the heart of members of the Diocese of Madison.

Happy St. Raphael's Feast Day!

Chapter Three: Holy Rosary

The Feast of the Most Holy Rosary originated in 1571 after a coalition of outnumbered papal forces called the Holy League defeated a huge Turkish fleet which attempted to invade Europe. If the Turks had won, the history of Christianity in Europe would surely have been different. This was a real crisis.

The crisis was so grave that Pope Saint Pius V ordered the churches of Rome stay open for prayer day and night. He encouraged the faithful gathered there to petition the intercession of the Blessed Virgin Mary through the recitation of the Rosary for victory. When word of the victory of the Holy League reached Pope Pius V he added the feast of Our Lady of Victory to the Roman Liturgical Calendar. Pope Pius V was not applauding the carnage of the battle but was grateful that Christians were still free to follow Jesus. He firmly believed that the triumph of the Holy League was due to Mary's intercession. Gregory XIII, Pope Pius V's successor changed the name of this day to the feast of the Holy Rosary.

This feast invites us to reflect upon the Rosary's mysteries. Through the Rosary's joyful, luminous, sorrowful and glorious mysteries, we review the story of our redemption. Pope Paul VI once called the Rosary a form of spiritual television during which we try to visualize each mystery as we pray the Hail Marys.

According to the National Bishop's Conference, the Rosary is a Scripture-based prayer. It begins with the Apostles Creed which summarizes the great mysteries of the Catholic faith. The Our Father is from the gospels. (The Glory Bes praise and acknowledge our Triune God.) The first part of the Hail Mary contains the angel's words announcing Christ's birth and Elizabeth's greeting to Mary. Pope Pius V officially added the second part of the Hail Mary when we ask Mary 53 times to pray for us now and at the hour of our death.

The Rosary's repetition can lead us into restful and contemplative prayer related to each Mystery. The gentle repetition of the words helps us to enter into the silence of our hearts, where Christ's spirit dwells.

The Rosary can be said privately or with a group. When I visited Fr. Joe Bricklin, Waunakee, he excused himself by saying "It's time to pray the Rosary, I pray it alone." I like to pray in a group because Jesus said, "Where two or three are gathered in my name, I am in their midst."

Father Joseph Krempa wrote, "Many prisoners of war have remarked that they prayed the Rosary in their cells by using the fingers of their hands. Doing so helped them maintain sanity and hope." He added that the Rosary's beauty is that it is a prayer for all people of every culture, the young who cannot yet read, the elderly, and everyone in between. It is also a prayer for spiritual victory over temptations in our life and the evils of our time.

Today we have our own battles to fight. There is the violence of terrorism and war. There is economic war, cultural war, political war, racial war, and spiritual war. Cleverly packaged secular atheistic humanism which denies our need for God may tempt us to follow its ways. We are all involved in some way in a war for the soul of our culture.

October can remind us of Venerable Father Patrick Peyton, the Rosary priest. He was an Irish Roman Catholic priest and promoter of the Rosary. He founded the "Family Rosary Crusade." He staged massive Rosary rallies in key cities of the world and extensively used mass communication. World-recognized celebrities of Hollywood especially during the mid 1900's helped promote his ministry of binding families through prayer under the Family Rosary. Celebrities included Loretta Young, Gregory Peck, Bing Crosby and others. Father Peyton was a popular and charismatic figure in Latin America and the Philippines where he promoted the Rosary and was known for his strong Irish accent

He popularized the phrases, "The family that prays together stays together" and "A world at prayer is a world at peace."

Chapter Four: Fall of Our Lives

1: Retirement Has Its Blessings, Challenges

On July 22, 2013, during the flight to World Youth Day, Pope Francis said that "Youth are the future." He quickly added that the aged are also essential.

He stated that he did not want World Youth Day to be a meeting with young people in isolation because when we isolate them, we do them an injustice.

Like us, he said, they belong to a family, a culture, a country, and faith. To know who we are, and where we are going, it's helpful to know where we came from.

Everyone is Welcome

Pope Francis said, "What the world needs now is a culture of inclusion and encounter to make sure that everyone's place and contribution to society is welcomed." As a high school teacher of 22 years and a baseball coach of 42 years, I respect the young.

Pope Francis said, "The young are the future because they are strong, but they are not the only keys to a healthy future for a society, nation, or world. Sometimes we set the elderly aside as if they have nothing to give, but they have the wisdom of life, history of our homelands and families, that we need."

Seniors Have Much to Offer

I agree, but I think that some seniors can offer even more than Pope Francis mentions. Each senior citizen is different. Some suffer from poor health, need physical assistance, and memory care. On the other hand, other senior citizens are in reasonably good health and mentally alert. These include our 76-year-old pope and many retired priests.

Ronald Reagan, Pope John XXIII, and Pablo Casals influenced many when they were in their late 70s.

Pablo Casals, the great cellist, believed that we have a responsibility to work together for peace. At age 84, he promoted peace by performing his oratorio "The Manger" all over the world. He continued this as he grew older. He said that his contribution to peace was small, but he gave all that he could. On the other hand, an 85-year-old is still 85. But let's not bury alive those who are still fully alive.

Retired Priests

I've seen priests in their 80s celebrate Mass with energy and enthusiasm while others struggle, and some find offering Mass physically difficult and even impossible.

The following description of retired priests on the Diocese of

Madison vocation website illustrates this: "The word retirement brings about the connotation that one's work has come to an end. That might be a good definition in mainstream society, but when one examines the life of a retired priest, they find that the priest is just as busy, or sometimes, busier than he was before retirement!"

"In the Diocese of Madison, priests are required to submit a retirement letter to the bishop when they have reached 70 years of age. The bishop may grant them a retirement at that time, or, if they are able and willing, he may ask the priest to remain active until a successor to his parish can be appointed. Dioceses that experience a priest shortage are more likely to keep priests in active ministry until well past the age of 70 years.

"Once in retirement, priests very often continue to serve in their home diocese, and sometimes in other dioceses as well. Many of the retired priests in the Diocese of Madison assist our active clergy with weekday and weekend Mass obligations and other duties as their schedules allow.

"The Bless Our Priests Fund continues to provide for the needs of our retired clergy, to ensure that they are well cared for in thanksgiving for all that they have done and have given to the Church and her people in the Diocese of Madison."

Value of Priests

This inspiring description of retired priests shows that like Pope Francis, the Madison Diocese concretely values not only senior citizens, but senior citizens who are retired priests. A retired priest enjoys retirement's blessings. He no longer has responsibilities for maintenance, countless meetings, endless ringing phones, multiple appointments, or pressures of running a parish. If he is called upon, there is more quality time to prepare homilies.

Retirement Challenges

The challenges of retirement vary with each priest. Challenges that I've experienced include downsizing, apartment living, and occasional lack of "help-outs."

There is also the unexpected, which may include health and other present and future crosses. Sometimes during retirement, it seems I've had to make almost as many adjustments as a chiropractor on a busy day, but grace helped me survive.

Fr. Mychal Judge, who died in the tragedy of September 11, 2001, was quoted posthumously, "If you want to make God laugh, tell him what you're going to do tomorrow!" A teammate on our losing sophomore football team often said, "Wait'll next year!" Next year or tomorrow may never come! At least it didn't for us.

I'm grateful that God called me to priesthood. The prayers and support of family, friends, and others were channels of grace that helped me to persevere and enjoy retirement.

2: Caring for the Dying in the Death-Denying Society

Mother Teresa claimed that the greatest disease of the modern world is not leprosy or cancer. Rather it is feeling unloved and unwanted. So, she and her nuns went into India's streets and picked up the dying and ministered to them. Though many died shortly after, she wanted them to experience Christ's love before they died.

Death-Denying Society

Dr. Elisabeth Kubler-Ross believed that we live in a death-denying society. We isolate and institutionalize the dying and elderly because they remind us of our mortality. We could give families more help with home care and visiting nurses. We should give families and patients spiritual, emotional, and financial help.

God Answers Prayers

Cicely Saunders, hospice's foundress, showed that God can use the most unlikely persons to accomplish good. As a teenager, she embraced atheism. Then after years of unhappiness and searching, she had a profound experience of God and became a Christian. Changed by God's love, she daily prayed this brave prayer, "Lord, what do I have to do today to thank you and to serve you?"

God's answer came when Cicely became a medical social worker and cared for David Tasma, a refugee from Poland's Warsaw ghetto. Abandoned by family and friends, he was dying alone in a large London hospital. At age 40, he felt that his life made no difference. Their professional relationship turned into a deep friendship. Together they spun dreams of creating more homelike places where people could spend their last days with dignity. When David died, on February 25, 1948, he left Cicely a gift of £500 and this encouraging note: "Let me be a window in your home."

Caring for the Dying

After David's death, Cicely decided to learn more about caring for the dying. First, she worked as a volunteer at St. Luke's Home for the Dying. Then she decided to study medicine. She became a doctor at age 38.

Eventually Cicely established St. Christopher's Hospice. There she developed a systematic approach of pain control for dying patients. She also gave attention to their social, emotional, and spiritual needs.

She offered a positive alternative that sought to ensure pain relief, maintain dignity, and bring tranquility to the dying. Her motto was, "You matter because you are you, and you matter until the last moment of your life. We will do all we can to help you, not only to die peacefully, but to live until you die."

Hospice exists in the hope and belief that through appropriate care and the promotion of a caring community sensitive to the dying person's needs, patients and families will be helped during the process of dying.

3: Visiting the Nursing Home is a Sacred Ministry

A nursing home is a holy place. It is a sacred space because it is home for the aged and handicapped who need special love and care. They also need the gift of our visits. When we visit them, we show that we care about them.

A painting depicts a long line of people patiently waiting to be fed at a soup kitchen. Over the head of one of them is a halo. This person is Jesus. If we look carefully, we may notice that Jesus is smiling. This painting reminds us that when we help someone in need, we help Jesus. We may even make him smile.

Pope John Paul II stressed the importance of visiting the elderly when he said, "I express deep appreciation to all those persons who find the time and the way to approach and assist the elderly who are most in need because they are abandoned or forgotten. Christian faith helps us to see the face of Jesus in the person in need."

Pope John Paul's remarks remind us that when we visit a person in a nursing home, we visit Jesus. We respect the nursing home resident as a unique person created in God's image. We listen attentively even if we have heard the story before. Listening is an act of love which shouts that we care. It allows the nursing home resident to relive the story or share current thoughts.

We can also read to residents, write letters, share our favorite Bible passage, pray with them or share stories of the good old days.

Between Generations

Most residents love visitors who are children. Such visits can be teachable moments for the children and visitors. I remember an elderly lady who lit up like a Christmas tree when she was visited by her great grandchild. "Bambino, bambino," she shouted enthusiastically. Suddenly she seemed 30 years younger.

We can invite children to draw and bring their masterpieces to residents to brighten their room and spirits, A Non-Catholic resident told me that she studied the drawing of Jesus on the crucifix that children made out of an egg box. In a voice of suffering, she told me that she decided not to complain anymore. I was deeply moved.

We can share news about our family and ask them about theirs. We can bring a photo album or work with them on a common project. A resident named Marge and I collaborated on making a poster entitled Beatitudes for the Aged. She received permission to proudly display it in her nursing home.

If the staff approves and the residents are up to it, we might share lunch, a drive, ice cream, beauty parlor, or a parade. As we do so, we should enjoy it too. If we cannot visit, we can call, or send a card or note.

Bringing, Receiving Love

We can say hello to other residents who may not receive many visitors. This brightens their day and enables us to observe another resident's care. Perhaps we can occasionally thank those who work faithfully in nursing homes. They deserve it.

Whether we are a new or a veteran visitor, we can check with the nursing home for visiting guidelines and tips for improving visiting skills.

When we visit, we often receive more than we give. We discover that the residents are survivors. They have survived heartbreak, deaths of loved ones, illnesses, and near death. They share gifts of faith, humor, understanding, wisdom, and friendship. Their experiences are written with grace on their faces and in stories they long to share.

Some of the residents are frail and forgotten and linger like the last leaf of autumn on the tree of loneliness. They long for visitors who seldom come and who never stay. Perhaps their family or friends are dead or live too far away. A compassionate visitor can help them to live with their cross of loneliness.

Others are regularly visited by children, friends, or other Christians. I am often touched by their loyalty and love. Some residents are so frail and weak that all they can do is pray. We can pray with them and invite them to make their suffering redemptive by uniting it with the suffering of Jesus.

Nursing home residents offer a preview of life that we may someday experience. They appreciate our visits. So does Jesus. At the judgment, pray that Christ will say to nursing home visitors, "When I was lonely in a nursing home, you visited me. Enter into the fullness of eternal life."

A nursing home is a sacred place because special people live and work there. To be a visitor requires a faithful response to a special grace. Perhaps such a person is you. If you become a visitor, you may make Jesus smile. And its benefits are heavenly.

4: Remember the Elderly in the Autumn of Their Lives

October 1 is International Day of Older Persons as declared by the United Nations. It is appropriate to celebrate this day during the fall of the year in order to focus upon the elderly's autumn blessings and needs. An elderly Italian couple reminded me of this recently.

Visiting the Elderly

On August 9, 2016, in Rome, Italy, four policemen visited the home of Michele, a 94-year-old man and Jole, his 89-year-old wife. After 70 years of marriage, they still loved each other, but they were suffering from the cross of loneliness, partially because their neighbors were vacationing and also because of upsetting TV reports about terrorists' attacks and abused children.

To comfort them, the officers cooked the couple's favorite Italian meal – spaghetti with butter and parmesan. They also spent the evening socializing with them and learning about their lives. The officers posted the couples' cross of loneliness on Facebook. In the post, they wrote poetically, "Life isn't always easy, especially when the city empties and neighbors are away on holiday. Sometimes loneliness dissolves into tears. Sometimes it's like a summer storm that suddenly overwhelms you."

According to the U. S. Department of Health and Human Services, by 2060, there will be about 98 million older Americans, more than twice their number in 2014. According to a University of California, San Francisco study, 43 percent of elderly people feel lonely, but only 18 percent live alone.

Alone and Unloved

This shows that loneliness doesn't necessarily come from being alone, but from feeling alone and unloved because nobody seems to care. Being loved helps to give meaning and purpose to life. I know! In an October 1, 2013 interview, Pope Francis stated that youth unemployment and the elderly's loneliness were "the most urgent problems facing the Church." He added, "The old need care and companionship; the young need employment."

In 1994 in a speech at the National Prayer Breakfast in Washington, D.C., St. Teresa said, "I remember visiting a home for elderly parents of children who had put them there and maybe forgot them. They had good food, comfortable quarters, television, and other necessities; but everyone kept looking towards the door. I asked, 'Sister, why are these people who have every comfort, always looking towards the door? Why aren't they smiling? I'm accustomed to seeing even the dying smile.'

"Sister explained, 'They are hoping that a son or daughter will come to visit them. They are hurt because they are forgotten."

Reaching Out

Bobbie Smith, a recognized professional caregiver for Home Instead

Senior Care, offers some doable ways we can respond to lonely elderly persons.

- Visit them and keep in touch. Listen and observe. Smile, even if it hurts. Asking them to "tell me more" is a simple way to get them and ourselves to open up.
- Be ready to respond to the unexpected. Smith walked with a grumpy, withdrawn 91-year-old man. She began to sing "Let me Call You Sweetheart." Unexpectedly the angry man began to sing with her and spoke to her for the first time when he reluctantly acknowledged, "you're okay!"
- Research shows that unrecognized elderly adults experience cognitive decline at much faster rates than seniors who are mentally stimulated by relationships.
- Invite the elderly to share their hard-earned wisdom, knowledge, and humor. Foster relationships between seniors and younger persons.
- Do something simple such as sending cards, bringing little gifts, or their favorite snack. These and other loving gestures help seniors feel they aren't throwaways, but human persons.

Giving Time

For those of you who go the extra mile for the elderly, keep up your graced work! When I was in assisted living, a 97-year-old man said that regular visits by his three daughters kept him going.

Perhaps there are elderly persons, including invisible or forgotten relatives, who would appreciate a friend, telephone call, or visit. Being a friend can help prevent loneliness. Are we willing and able to make or take time to be that friend? Let's remember that it's in the family that we learned to respect and care for others, especially the elderly who once cared for us. Now maybe it's our turn to give back to them.

Chapter Five: All Saints & All Souls Day

1: Let's Respond To Our Call To Be Saints

In the novel, The Power and the Glory, Graham Greene describes a priest who ministered to Catholics during a religious persecution in

Mexico. Fear of being caught by the police and the exhausting work of serving his people finally took its toll. He becomes an alcoholic. He was imprisoned and awaited execution.

Shortly before his execution, he wept not because he was afraid to die, but because he feared going to God empty-handed. It seemed to him that it would have been easy to be a saint. He just needed a little more self-restraint and courage. He felt like someone who missed happiness by seconds at an appointed place. He knew now that the only thing that ultimately mattered was to be a saint.

Phyllis McGinley was a 1961 Pulitzer Prize-winning American author of children's books and poetry. She also wrote a book entitled *Saint Watching*. In the book she wrote, "When I was seven years old, I wanted to become a tight rope walker until I broke my collarbone practicing on a child's-size high wire. At twelve I planned to become an international spy. At fifteen my ambition was the stage. Now in my declining years I would give anything to be a saint." Her words hint at her humorous, down-to-earth, yet beautiful journey to adult faith.

Phyllis McGinley's remarks remind us that without exception each of us is called to be a saint. In No. 2013 of the Catechism of the Catholic Church, it says, "All Christians in any state or walk of life are called to the fullness of Christian life and to the perfection of charity. All are called to holiness: Be perfect, as your heavenly Father is perfect."

We honor canonized saints on specific days of the church year; but we honor uncanonized saints on All Saints Day. Countless men, women and children are united with God in heavenly glory. They are alluded to in Revelation 7:9 in the first reading of All Saints Day where it says, "A great multitude that no one could count, from every nation, from all tribes and peoples and languages, was standing before the throne and before the Lamb, robed in white, with palm branches in their hands."

We can compare uncanonized saints to the Unknown Soldier. We know that the Unknown Soldier represents many unsung heroes, but we don't know who they were because their song was never known, recognized or sung publicly.

Some saints seemed holy all their lives. Others were sinners who experienced conversion's miracle of grace. They include St. Paul who persecuted Christians, Margaret of Cortonna, the Mary Magdalen of the Middle Ages, St. Camillus of the fiery temper and many others. They offer hope that if they are in Heaven, then maybe we can get there too.

Padre Pio said, "It's difficult to become a saint, but not impossible. The road to perfection is long, as long as one's lifetime. Along the way, consolation becomes rest; but soon as your strength is restored, you must diligently get up and resume the trip."

The saints lived and sometimes died for Christ. When Jesus said to give up everything and live for the poor, St. Francis and others responded wholeheartedly, because Jesus their Savior, was calling them. They needed his grace to respond.

We probably aren't called to lay down our life for Christ as a martyr, but we are called to lay down our life for Christ daily in little ways that take courage and perseverance. In No. 825 of the Catechism of the Catholic Church it says, "All the faithful, whatever their condition and state -though each in his own way- are called by the Lord to the perfection of sanctity by which the Father himself is perfect."

A once popular banner read, "Bloom where you are planted." This means that if you are a parent, at this moment in your life, God wants you to be a saint by being the best parent you can be. That's what Mary did.

If you are a student, God wants you to be the best student that you can be, as St. Thomas Aquinas was.

If you are an elderly couple, God intends you to be a saint, by being the best elderly couple you can be, like Joachim and Anne!

I enjoy asking children who reminds them of Jesus. They often say, "Grandma, Grandpa, Mom, Dad, friends, a teacher and once in a while my priest." They may be part of the crowd of uncanonized saints whom we honor on All Saints Day.

A married lady told me that part of her vocation is to help her family get to Heaven. I agree! As the priest and Phyllis McGinley said, the only thing that ultimately matters is being a saint now so we can enjoy Heaven forever with God, the angels and saints. God offers us grace to become a saint. Let's respond to this grace every day but especially on All Saints Day.

2: November Reminds Us to Pray for a Happy Death

During November we celebrate All Saints Day, All Souls Day, and the Feast of Christ the King. We also begin Advent when we focus upon Christ's Second Coming and prayerfully, patiently await his birth.

All Saints Day is a solemn holy day which we celebrate on November. On All Saints Day the Catholic Church honors those who have died and are in Heaven and who have lived heroic Christ like lives in response to God's grace. On All Saints Day we honor uncanonized saints of the Catholic church who have lived a Christ-like life.

To be recognized as a canonized saint of the Catholic church one has to go through a lengthy process. The church makes a lengthy examination of the person's life to see if he or she is a person of heroic virtue. If successful, he or she is given the title of Venerable, a title which Father Samuel Mazzuchelli has. Canonization does not put a person in Heaven. It just recognizes that he or she is already there.

Though some say that we live in a society that tries to deny death; nevertheless, we will die. November's feasts remind us to pray for the grace of a happy death. A happy death means dying peacefully in a state of grace so we can meet our Lord with great joy upon dying. In Wisdom 3:1,3, it says, "The souls of the just are in the hands of God and the torment of death shall not touch them, they are in peace." This passage is often read at funeral Masses.

Despite intense suffering, the Venerable Father Samuel who was born on November 3, 1806 and who served in what is now our diocese, died courageously with happy thoughts. In Acts 10:38 it says that Jesus went about doing good. So did Fr. Samuel. He worked for social justice for the Indians, helped the poor and contributed to the common good. Father Mazzuchelli died as he lived, ministering to others.

On February 15, 1864, an old woman who lived out on the prairie requested the last sacraments. Like Pope Francis, Father Mazzuchelli rushed to give her the last rites. When he returned to St. Patrick's, he experienced a chill. Physicians were called and he was diagnosed as having pleura pneumonia. For the next week the Sinsinawa Dominican Sisters whom he founded took turns sitting by his bedside. Since he had difficulty breathing, he had to sit up in bed. The day before he died, he exclaimed, "O good Mother." Tears of joy rolled down his cheeks. He explained to the puzzled Sisters that he was joyful because he had been on a long, painful journey, separated from family and friends. Now he caught a glimpse of his Heavenly home. He asked his puzzled care giving Sisters, "Wouldn't you be joyful, too if you were nearing home (as I am?)," Shortly before he died, he prayed the Quam Dilecta (Psalm 84) which is inscribed on his gravestone.

His heroic sacrifices, long fasts, illnesses and hardships were not enough to offer to God. After his death, a penance chain was found on his body.

To a much greater degree, Mary does good for us on earth by interceding for us from Heaven. We recognize this when we pray "Holy Mary, mother of God, pray for us sinners now and at the hour of our death." When we pray the rosary, we ask Mary to pray for us 53 times now and at the hour of our death. St. Joseph, Mary's spouse, is also the patron saint of a happy death.

November invites us to pray for the Poor Souls in Purgatory so that they may be loosed from their sins and experience the Beatific Vision. All Saints Day invites us to live a Christ-like life and pray for the grace of dying peacefully in a state of grace so we can joyfully meet our Lord upon dying and enjoy our Heavenly home forever. Enjoy the gift of today!

3: A Catholic Cemetery is Holy Ground

We Catholics believe that a cemetery is holy ground because it is where the body rests until it is reunited with the soul at resurrection.

Caring for a cemetery requires skill and grace. I learned this as a boy and even more as a pastor. As a seventh and eighth grader, I mowed the school and church lawns of Kieler's Immaculate Conception Parish with a walking power mower. I was glad when the July the Fourth picnic came because picnic patrons tromped down the grass and made the lawn easier to mow.

I also shoveled coal in the church furnace. Hopefully I won't have to shovel it in eternity.

I also mowed the Immaculate Conception Parish cemetery for two years with the somewhat reluctant help of Herb, my brother.

Part of the reason for his reluctance was because two or three times each summer we clipped the grass around every tombstone. Our hand clippers were powered by elbow grease. This created blisters which I still feel. Today's new-fangled power trimmers were not available.

Herb remembers the bumblebees and gophers who thought they owned the cemetery. The money we earned went to our parents to help make ends meet. My brother and I had little or no spending money.

History in a Cemetery

As Herb and I clipped around the gravestones, I discovered that much personal history is buried in a cemetery, I studied the names especially of my grandparents, other relatives, and persons I knew. My grandparents on both sides of the family were buried in the cemetery. I did not realize then that mowing the cemetery was sacred work.

I always enjoyed discussing cemeteries with the late Donald Brandt, who cared for the Kieler cemetery for years. Today, the Kieler cemetery has a new section. Whenever I visit it, it seems like the old neighborhood. I could tell stories about many who are buried there. Two fervent baseball fans are buried closest to the baseball diamond. Maybe Dad and Uncle Will should also have been buried there because they were arguably Kieler's most zealous baseball fans.

When I became a pastor at age 56, the first thing I did was to start a cemetery committee at St. Patrick, Benton. A parishioner made a map. Others laid out the graves for the cemetery's new section. We also updated cemetery rules, which are necessary, but they can be touchy because survivors are concerned about their loved ones' graves and may occasionally stretch cemetery rules. At Ridgeway-Barneveld, I also helped to start a cemetery committee.

Caring for a Cemetery

Caring for a cemetery, especially a small cemetery, is interesting, challenging, and full of stories.

Whenever he passed a cemetery, the late Fr. Al Schubiger prayed. On my way to Darlington, I always stop at Belmont's St. Philomena Cemetery to pray at Fr. Monte Robinson's grave, which is integrated with an inspiring statue of the Pieta.

Sr. Nona McGreal, OP, who prepared the Positio for Venerable Fr. Samuel Mazzuchelli's possible canonization and wrote books about him, once asked if I would consider correcting the spelling error on the Benton cemetery sign. It was incorrectly spelled "Cemetary." I visualized scores of teaching Sisters who visited Father Mazzuchelli's grave and noticed the misspelling,

At the National Catholic Cemetery Conference workshop at Sinsinawa Mound, I mentioned this misspelling to the priest-president of the conference. He said that he thought this happens because of confusion with the word seminary. Cemeteries try to build up the perpetual care fund and use the interest gained from the principal to help maintain the graves, pay for mowing, and for the unexpected and other expenses.

Dealing with Changes

Tombstones, like cars, change in style. In the 1800s' there were some iron cross markers, a few iron monuments, and some marble tombstones.

At Benton, I liked the older white marble tombstones and tried to clean the moss or fungus off them. But unfortunately, with time, their resurrected white beauty would become covered with fungus again. They also are more brittle than granite and vandals can do more damage to them.

Upright marble tombstones are less common today because the big ones can be dangerous and over time inscriptions become difficult to read or even become unreadable.

Since the funeral Mass is about our hope for heaven, a religious symbol such as a cross, a rosary, or a Bible is appropriate for the tombstone. A symbol of the deceased life's work that expresses how they used their time, talents, and treasure to help to bring about God's kingdom and make this world a bit better is also fitting.

Every time I visit Benton's St. Patrick, I park my car near the grave of the Venerable Fr. Samuel Mazzuchelli and the graves of some of the first Dominican Sisters he founded. I visit their graves and say a quick prayer. May we continue to pray for the dead when we pass or visit a cemetery.

A lot of history is buried there. Sharing stories of the deceased helps us connect the past with the present and future.

4: November Reminds Us to Use the Gift of Time Wisely

In 1972 Jim Croce recorded the song, "Time in a Bottle." The lyrics of the song that especially spoke to me were, "But there never seems to be enough time to do the things you want to do, once you find them." These words seemed prophetic. Jim Croce was killed in a plane accident on September 20, 1973.

Jim Croce's death or any death reminds us of the fragility of life. Death reminds us Catholics that we are pilgrims on a journey through time to Eternity. Earth is our temporary home. Heaven is our Eternal Home. St. Paul urges us to run the race of life for the prize of Eternal Glory.

At the Judgment, Christ will ask us if we have been responsible stewards of the gift of life that God has given to us. Hopefully we will respond, "Yes, Lord. I have used your gifts of time, talent, and treasure to help to bring about the Kingdom of God." And we pray that Jesus responds, "Well done, good and faithful servant, enter into the fullness of Eternal life."

Focus on "Last Things"

During November the Church invites us to focus upon last things which pertain to our Eternal destiny – Death, Judgment, Heaven, Hell, Purgatory, and the Second Coming of Jesus.

We begin November on All Saints Day when, according to Pope Urban IV, we honor all saints, known and unknown. The saints remind us that we who are baptized are called to holiness. The example of their lives can inspire us to follow Jesus as they did. On All Saints Day especially, we ask our brothers and sisters in Heaven to pray to God for us.

Praying for All Souls

On All Souls Day we join the saints in Heaven in praying for our brothers and sisters in Purgatory. In Paragraph 1032 of the Catechism of the Catholic Church, it is stated, "From the beginning, the Church has honored the memory of the dead and offered prayers in suffrage for them, above all the Eucharistic sacrifice so that thus purified, they may attain the Beatific Vision of God."

On All Souls Day the Church also invites us to visit our parish cemetery, the final resting place for the body until it is reunited with the soul at the resurrection. We may obtain a plenary indulgence when we devoutly visit a cemetery and pray, even if only mentally, for the departed from November 1 to 8. This indulgence is applicable only to the Souls in Purgatory.

We conclude the Sundays of the Church year by celebrating the Feast of Christ the king. This feast reminds us that we will be judged on how well we spent the gift of our life to help to bring about God's kingdom of justice, love, and mercy!

All Saints Day reminds us that each time we pray the "Hail Mary," we ask the Blessed Mother to pray for us now and at the hour of our death. This reminds us, too, that St. Joseph, Mary's spouse, is the patron saint of a happy death. Among other things, a happy death means meeting our Lord in death in a state of grace, ready and eager to give a joyful, responsible accounting of our stewardship of the gift of our life to Him.

The day after we end the current Church year of Cycle A Scripture Mass readings, we immediately begin Cycle B readings of the next Church year by beginning the season of Advent when we focus upon waiting for the coming of Jesus and repeat the cycle.

Particular and Last Judgment

November's emphasis on last things reminds us that we will die. When we die, our soul will depart from our body and appear before our Lord in the Particular Judgment. In paragraph 1038 of the Catechism of the Catholic Church, it is stated that the resurrection of all the dead will precede the Last Judgment when our body will be reunited with our soul. The unjust "will go away into Eternal punishment but the righteous into Eternal Life." In paragraph 1058 of the Catechism it is stated that the Church prays that no one should be lost.

On the glorious Feast of Christ the King, we rejoice that Christ is enthroned at the right hand of the Father as Judge and King. We show that we have honored him as King by treating others as we would treat Jesus himself. By so doing we hope to hear Jesus' heavenly words, "Come, you have my Father's blessing; inherit the full of the kingdom."

The song "Time in a Bottle" and Jim Croce's early unexpected death remind us that our lives are enclosed in a fragile bottle of time. We believers pray for grace to make time to do the things God wants us to do.

We do this aided by the Holy Spirit who helps us to discern God's will for us, November reminds us that the way we use our time now can determine how we spend forever. Let us use it wisely. In the song, "Amazing Grace" are the words, "And grace will lead me home." Our hope is that by responding to grace, we will be welcomed into our Heavenly Home. This is Good News!

5: Christ Heals Through Sacrament of Sick

On August 4, 2013, a 19-year-old girl named Katie Lentz got in a serious accident along a Missouri highway. She was barely clinging to life, and her vital signs were fading when she asked rescue workers to pray with her. Suddenly a priest appeared from nowhere. A rescue worker welcomed him with the words, "Father, we need all the help we can get now!"

The priest prayed, anointed the girl, and gave her absolution. Fire Chief Raymond Reed said that after the anointing, a peaceful calmness seemed to come over the girl and rescue workers. When he turned to thank the priest, he was gone.

The unknown priest became known as the angel or mystery priest. Eventually his identity was discovered. His name is Fr. Patrick Dowling. He told ABC News, "I have no doubt the Most High answered the prayers of Katie and the rescue workers. I was part of God's answer, but only part." Katie survived and is in the long process of recovering.

Christ's Healing Ministry

During his earthly life, Jesus healed sick persons. The Church continues Christ's healing ministry through the Sacrament of the Anointing of the Sick (formerly known as Extreme Unction).

In No. 1511 of the Catechism of the Catholic Church, it says, "This sacred Anointing of the Sick was instituted by Christ our Lord as a true and proper sacrament. It is alluded to indeed by Mark but is recommended to the faithful and promulgated by James, the apostle."

In James 5:14-15 it says, "Is anyone among you sick? He should summon the presbyters of the Church and they will pray over him and anoint him with oil in the name of the Lord. This prayer of faith will save the sick person and the Lord will raise him up. If he has committed any sins, he will be forgiven."

In No. 1514 of the Catechism of the Catholic Church, it says, "The Anointing of the Sick is not a sacrament for those only who are at the point of death. Hence, as soon as anyone of the faithful begins to be in danger of death from sickness or old age, the fitting time for him to receive this sacrament has certainly already arrived."

In No. 1529 of the Catechism of the Catholic Church, it says, "Each time a Christian fall seriously ill, he may receive the Anointing of the Sick and also when, after he receives it, the illness worsens."

In No. 1513 of the Catechism of the Catholic Church, it says, "The Sacrament of the Anointing of the Sick is given to those who are seriously ill by anointing them on the forehead and hands with duly blessed oil – pressed from olives or from other plants – saying only once, 'Through this holy anointing may the Lord in his love and mercy help you with the grace of the Holy Spirit. May the Lord who frees you from sin save you and raise you up.'"

Practices Restored

The Anointing of the Sick gradually became known as Extreme Unction because it was often received by persons close to death. In the liturgical reforms that occurred after the Second Vatican Council, the original practice of anointing people with serious illnesses which were not necessarily life-threatening was restored.

In No. 1515 of the Catechism of the Catholic Church, it says, "If a sick person who received this anointing recover, he can in case of another grave illness receive this sacrament again. If during the same illness, the person's condition becomes more serious, the sacrament may be repeated. It is fitting to receive the Sacrament of the Sick just prior to a serious operation. The same holds true for the elderly whose frailty becomes more pronounced."

Before his death from cancer, Cardinal Joseph Bernardin was anointed several times.

Effects of the Sacrament

In No. 1532 of the Catechism of the Catholic Church, it says, "The special grace of the Sacrament of the Anointing of the Sick has as its effects:

"The uniting of the sick person to the passion of Christ, for his own good and that of the whole Church.

"The strengthening, peace, and courage to endure in a Christian manner the sufferings of illness or old age.

"The forgiveness of sins, if the sick person was not able to obtain it through the Sacrament of Penance.

"The restoration of health, if it is conducive to the salvation of his soul."

No. 1523 of the Catechism of the Catholic Church reads, "If the Sacrament of Anointing of the Sick is given to all who suffer from serious illness and infirmity, even more rightly is it given to those at the point of departing this life. The Anointing of the Sick completes our conformity to the death and Resurrection of Christ, just as baptism began it.

"It completes the holy anointings that mark the whole Christian life: that of baptism which sealed the new life in us, and that of Confirmation which strengthened us for the combat of this life. This last anointing fortifies the end of our earthly life like a solid rampart for the final struggles before entering the Father's house."

The Church also offers those who are about to leave this life the Eucharist as viaticum. In No. 1524 of the Catechism of the Catholic Church, it says, "Receiving Communion at this moment of 'passing over' to the Father has a particular significance and importance. It is the seed of eternal life and the power of resurrection, according to the words of the Lord: 'He who eats my flesh and drinks my blood has eternal life, and I will raise him up at the last day.'" Alleluia!

6: All Saints Day – All Believers are Called to Holiness

Occasionally I ask second and third graders to name someone who is kind, loving, forgiving, and reminds them of Jesus. Often, they reply grandma, grandpa, mom, dad, teacher, coach, friend, priest, sibling, sister, or someone else. The person whom they name may be one of the countless uncanonized saints whom we honor on All Saints Day, November 1.

On All Saints Day, we honor the Church's canonized and uncanonized saints, Canonized saints are persons whom the Church, after thoroughly examining their lives, declares they are in heaven. Uncanonized saints are persons who lived Christ-like lives, but whom the Church does not officially recognize as saints. In No. 2013 of the

Catechism of the Catholic Church it says, "All Christians in any state or walk of life are called to the fullness of Christian life and to the perfection of charity. All are called to holiness: 'Be perfect, as your heavenly Father is perfect.'"

Communion of Saints

All Saints Day reminds us that we are members of the beautiful Communion of Saints, the spiritual union of all members of the Church, those on earth, in heaven, and in purgatory. Each member contributes to the good of all and shares in their welfare. We are united in Christ by bonds of love stronger than death. We pray for and support each other on earth and ask those in heaven to pray for us. On All Souls Day, November 2, as members of the Communion of Saints, we join those in heaven in praying that those in purgatory be purified of sin and enter heaven.

Answering Call to Holiness

Most Catholics are laity and their role is very important. They are called to make the world holy in ways which only the laity can. They are called in a special way to make the Church present and operative in those places and circumstances where only through them can it become the salt of the earth. Even when preoccupied with temporal cares, the laity can and must perform a work of great value for the evangelization of the world. By their combined efforts lay persons are called to remedy the customs and conditions of the world if they are an inducement to sin, so that all may be conformed to the norms of justice and may favor the practice of virtue rather than hinder it. By so doing they will imbue culture and human activity with genuine moral value (Vatican II, Constitution of Church in Modern World. Nos 33, 35, 36 and 37).

Canonized and uncanonized saints' lives are characterized by patience, respect, love, understanding, and other gifts and fruits of the Holy Spirit. Their Christ-like example inspires us to answer Jesus' call to holiness.

We Catholics who live our faith can enjoy the best of both worlds. We can be happier in this world and help to make it a better place as countless saints did. When we live a Christ-like life, we believe that for us, death is not the end, but the door to heaven, where, through

God's grace and mercy, we will enjoy God's presence face to face forever.

Chapter Six: Thanksgiving

1: Thanksgiving – One of God's Favorite Words

Mark Twain, the writer, reportedly once earned five dollars per word. Someone playfully wrote him, "Mr. Twain, here is five dollars. Please send me your favorite word." Mark Twain wrote back, "Thanks!"

Thanksgiving also is one of God's favorite words. The word Eucharist, the center of Catholic life, means thanksgiving.

In Luke 17:11-19, Jesus cured 10 lepers of leprosy's horrible disease, but only one leper, a Samaritan, thanked him. Jesus seemed hurt that the nine others did not thank him. Their ingratitude seems unbelievable, but there are similar examples.

Missed Opportunities

On September 8, 1860, on Lake Michigan near Waukegan, Ill., the Lady Elgin, an excursion boat, collided with a schooner, the Augusta. Edward Spencer, a Methodist seminarian, plunged into the cold waters and saved 17 people from drowning.

After he rescued the last two persons, he collapsed. His heroism ruined his health and eventually made him an invalid. Years later a reporter asked Edmund Spencer what he remembered most about his heroic rescues. He replied sadly that no one ever thanked him. The 17 persons reflected the ingratitude that the nine lepers showed to Jesus.

God has Gifted Us

We probably learn to be grateful from our parents. I opened the door at McDonald's for a mother carrying a little boy, "Thank you, sir," she said. Her little boy shouted, "Thank you sir, thank you." Gratitude begins when we see that God has gifted us. Then we respond by verbally thanking God or others. Or we share our blessings with others as the pilgrims did.

About half of the pilgrims died from scurvy and exposure to the elements during their first brutal winter in America. Yet, the survivors were so thankful they were alive that they invited Indian friends to share a three-day feast of thanksgiving and prayer.

Giving Thanks Through Times of Strife

Sometimes we fail to thank God for our blessings because we get so involved in activities that we forget about Jesus. St. Paul didn't. Despite being in prison, in Philippians 4:6, Paul joyfully prayed, "Present your needs to God in every form of prayer and in petitions full of gratitude." We begin our best prayers with praise and thanks to God.

Thanksgiving Day invites us to thank God for our blessings through prayer, thanking others, and sharing our blessings. Thanksgiving Day offers graced opportunities to thank family members. Dr. Nick Stinnett of the University of Nebraska did research which showed that families are stronger when members express appreciation to each other.

Since Eucharist means thanksgiving, we can thank God for our blessings by participating in a Thanksgiving Day Mass. We receive the body of Christ in order that we might be strengthened to give thanks by sharing with others. On Thanksgiving and every day may we remember that one of God's favorite words is ... thanks.

2: Thank God for Blessings Seen and Unseen

Thanksgiving's roots go back to the Pilgrims. After a long hard year during which more than half died from scurvy or exposure to the elements, survivors held a feast of thanksgiving during which they shared their blessings with Indian friends.

The Pilgrims thanked God that enough of them survived to start a new life for themselves and their descendants. As the colonies grew more prosperous, however, people tended to forget about Thanksgiving. Consequently, Thanksgiving was celebrated sporadically, if at all.

Effort to Restore Thanksgiving

Sarah Hale was a plucky widow, mother of five children, and editor of a woman's magazine. She wrote the nursery rhyme Mary had a Little Lamb.

In 1822, she began a 40-year campaign of writing editorials and letters to governors and presidents urging them to revive the celebration of Thanksgiving and restore it to its rightful place.

Three presidents turned her down. Eventually in 1863, President Abraham Lincoln proclaimed the last Thursday in November as an annual day of Thanksgiving. In some ways, Lincoln was an unlikely person to do so because he seemed to have little for which to be thankful. Many members of his cabinet openly despised him and joked about him publicly. His wife had been investigated as a possible traitor, a process that deeply wounded Lincoln.

Being Thankful for What We Have

Sometimes we can become more thankful for what we have when we see what others don't have. An anonymous author wrote, "If you woke up this morning and could hear the birds singing, use your vocal cords to utter human sounds, walk to breakfast and read the newspaper with two good eyes, you are more blessed than millions of people who cannot do such things."

If you have never experienced the danger of battle, the loneliness of temptation, the agony of torture, or the pangs of starvation, you are ahead of 500 million people in the world. If you can attend a church meeting without fear of harassment, arrest, or torture, then you are more blessed than three billion people in the world. If you have food in the refrigerator, clothes to wear, a roof overhead, and a place to sleep, you are richer than 75 per cent of the world.

Thank God for Our Blessings by Sharing Them with Others

The Gospel on the Feast of Christ the King (Sunday, Nov. 26) reminds us that we can thank God for our blessings by sharing them with our neighbor in need (Matthew 25:31-46).

Years ago, a salesman was reduced to living out of his car because he could not sell anything. He ate nothing for two days. He was so hungry that he walked into a diner and ordered breakfast. He was broke.

As he devoured his breakfast, he wondered how he would get out of paying for it. When the bill came, he told the waitress that he left his wallet in the car which was true, but he did not say there was no money in it.

The diner's owner had already sized him up and could see that he didn't have any money. The owner approached the salesman and bent down to pick up a piece of paper that the man had apparently dropped. Then he straightened up and growled at the broke salesman, "Sir, it looks as if you dropped this $20 bill. You should be more careful with your money!" He handed the man a $20 bill, winked, and fled to hide in the kitchen.

Thanks to the owner's generosity, the salesman now had enough money to pay for the breakfast, buy gas, as well as five loaves of bread and two pounds of butter. He never forgot this undeserved act of generosity and goodness. Since then, whenever he can, he tries to pass on the man's generosity to others, especially as a Secret Santa.

Since Eucharist means Thanksgiving, let us resolve to thank God by participating in Mass on Thanksgiving Day and whenever we can. May our Thanksgiving Day be filled with food, fellowship, gratitude, and love. May we continue to thank God every day for our blessings that we see and don't see yet!

Chapter Seven: Feast of Christ The King

Pope Pius XI established the feast of Christ the King as a worldwide feast in 1925. The pope added this feast to the church year to respond to growing secularism and to the waning faith in Christ the King by Catholics and others. Pope Pius XI hoped this feast would motivate Catholics and others to reject Godless ways and accept Christ as king and savior. Despite the end of World War One, "the war to end all wars", Pope Pius XI feared Godless philosophies that would lead to nationalism, dictatorships, wars and great suffering.

Pope Pius XI was prophetic. Despite some democracies in parts of Europe and the world, dictators ruled Germany, Russia, Italy, Mexico and other countries. These dictators exercised complete control over their subjects.

Karl Marx influenced communism; a Godless philosophy that made the state supreme. Communism seemed concerned for the poor, but once communists gained control, their effects were often devastating. Stalin butchered millions of his own people, Friedrich Nietzsche influenced Hitler and popularized the "God is dead" philosophy. Communism, Fascism and Nazism sought to banish Christ from public life. Hitler lowered genocide to inhuman lows. These philosophies helped to cause the World War Two nightmare. Estimates of total deaths caused by this war range from 50 million to more than 80 million. The higher figure of over 80 million includes deaths from war-related disease and famine.

Blessed Miguel Pro whose feast is November 23 can inspire us to follow Christ and celebrate the feast of Christ the king with fresh eyes. In 1925 Miguel Pro was a Jesuit seminarian in Mexico when there was a revolution which led to the church's persecution; consequently, he studied for priesthood in other countries. When he returned to Mexico as an ordained priest, Father Pro discovered that churches had been closed and priests were subject to arrest. His humor, imagination and faith helped him to become a master of disguises. He dressed himself as a beggar, businessman, dock worker, street sweeper and other disguises. One disguise enabled him to ask a police station for directions. On EWTN.com, Father Shannon M. Collins, stated that Blessed Miguel Pro, during one narrow escape from his pursuers, linked arms with a beautiful young girl whispering, "Help me, I'm a priest." The girl cooperated and the two pretended to be a couple on a date.

Using clever disguises Father Pro rode a bicycle administering Baptism, Holy Communion and Last Rites. He heard many confessions. He also took up collections to help the poor. Shortly before his martyrdom, Fr. Miguel offered Mass at a convent. He prophetically told the Mother Superior: "I offered my life for the saving of Mexico some time ago, Sister, and this morning at Mass I felt that He had accepted it."

According to Father Joseph Krempa, in an assassination attempt on the former president of Mexico, bomb throwers used an automobile that had been owned by the Pro family. The Pro brothers were arrested and falsely accused of the bombing attempt. There was no due process or trial. As Father Pro was led to his death, he blessed and forgave his executioners, knelt in front of a bullet pocked wall and prayed the rosary. Then he stood up, stretched out his arms, forming a cross with his body and shouted, "Viva Cristo Rey" as the bullets were fired. He was 36 years old.

The government invited newsmen to photograph the execution.

They thought this would deter others from disobeying the government. They were convinced the newsmen would photograph a coward. Instead their pictures revealed the death of a heroic martyr. Rather than a deterrent, Father Miguel's execution became an inspiration; consequently, the government immediately forbade anyone to have such a photo.

Fr. Miguel sought to keep the light of the faith alive until the nightmare of persecution passed. It's hard to believe that such a terrible persecution took place in Mexico, a heavily Catholic country bordering the United States.

Cleverly packaged secular values, the world, flesh, devil and weak faith can tempt some of us to follow worldly ways rather than Christ's ways. As Pius XI wrote in the encyclical Quas Primas, "On Christ's Kingship the world's manifold evils happen because the majority of men have thrust Jesus Christ and His Holy Law out of their lives …and as long as individuals and States refuse to submit to the rule of our Savior, there will be no hope for lasting peace. The only hope for the reign of peace and righteousness is to recognize Christ's reign in our hearts and to restore the Empire of Christ in our families - our cities – our nation – and yes in the universe."

May Blessed Miguel Pro's heroic example inspire us to follow Christ our king and Savior through time into Eternity. Let us pray that someday soon the Christ like lives of believers around the world will imitate Father Pro and cry out with one accord – Viva Cristo Rey – Long Live Christ the King!

PART VIII: FR. SAMUEL MAZZUCHELLI

1: Fr. Samuel Mazzuchelli – An Inspiration in The Year of Faith

Carlo Gaetano Samuel Mazzuchelli was born on November 4, 1806 in Milan, Italy. He died in 1864 as pastor of St. Patrick's, Benton. Years later, as pastor of St. Patrick's, I walked the parish grounds, presided at Mass, and visited his rectory and grave. My knowledge and admiration of him deepened. He certainly is an inspiration in this Year of Faith.

Father Samuel, a Dominican priest, accomplished so much that I get tired just thinking about it. A parishioner called him "our steam engine missionary." He was architect and builder of more than 20 churches. He believed deeply in God's Providence and venerated Mary. He designed and built civic buildings and helped to establish many parishes and schools. He was a master preacher and teacher who taught at Benton St. Clara Academy and other places.

He founded the Sinsinawa Dominican Sisters and served as chaplain of the first session of the Wisconsin Territorial Legislature.

He wrote memoirs of his life and mission and founded the Sinsinawa Mound College of St. Thomas Aquinas. He ministered to Wisconsin-Michigan Indians and wrote a liturgical almanac in Chippewa and a Winnebago Prayer book.

At Shullsburg settler's request, he named some of its streets Faith and Wisdom, Peace and Charity, Judgement and Truth, Friendship, Mercy, and Joy.

When I drive on Judgement St., I slow down and pray. Now I live next to the beautiful stone building that Father Mazzuchelli built at the Mound.

Caring for the Sick

In 1850 a cholera epidemic struck New Diggins, Wis. Senator James Earnest helped Father Samuel care for the sick. Susan, his daughter, wrote to Sr. Benedicta Kennedy, "I have heard my father tell of when there was an epidemic of cholera in New Diggings. Nearly every family was afflicted. Father Samuel and my father worked shoulder to shoulder, giving them (the afflicted) help and comfort."

Father Mazzuchelli transacted wills and bequests hastily made by dying Protestant and Catholic parents. He took responsibility for orphans. His mother died when he was six and some of his early classmates were orphans.

Protecting the Church

In 1862 when the Benton Primitive Methodist Church burned, Catholics were suspected. Father Samuel wrote to Thomas Bainbridge, elder of that Church, "I send $25.00 as my contribution for rebuilding the church destroyed by fire. My object in doing so is to convince all parties that the Catholic Church does condemn incendiaries under any excuse or pretext, political or religious." The $25 was greater than St. Patrick's total collections for six months.

Father Samuel died as he lived, praying and ministering to others. Wherever he served, no Catholic died without the sacraments. On February 15, 1864, he gave the last sacraments to Dennis Murphy, Benton's first settler. Then a dying woman requested the last sacraments. During the long ride to her sickbed, he experienced chills and severe pains. A physician diagnosed that he suffered from Pleroma pneumonia.

The following days two physician and his confessor attended him while Dominican Sisters kept an unbroken prayer vigil untied, he died on February 23, 1864, in Benton at age 57. News of his death spread throughout America.

Cause for Sainthood

Father Samuel helped to spiritually and physically build the Church where he served. After he died, many prayed for his canonization. On July 9, 1964, Mother Benedicta, Sinsinawa Dominican Prioress, formally petitioned for official establishment of the cause for his hoped-for beatification and canonization.

Under the direction of the Vatican Congregation for Causes of Saints, Dominican Sr. Nona McGreal wrote a formal presentation of his life and virtue (called a positio). The document's historical review was completed in 1990. Next expert theologians reviewed it to determine the heroic quality of his virtues.

On July 6, 1993, Fr Samuel Mazzuchelli was declared "Venerable" by Pope Johns Paul II. The title "Venerable" recognizes his holiness and completes the first step towards his canonization.

A Man of Sacrifice

Next, the Church examines reports of miraculous favors attributed to him. If a miracle is approved, the Pope would beatify Father Mazzuchelli with the title "Blessed."

If the Church approves a second miracle, Father Samuel could be honored by the Church as "Saint Samuel." This would make many hearts dance with joy!

In a Benton St. Patrick's pictorial directory, someone wrote, "Father Samuel was a man of great sacrifice. We marvel at his commitment to God and people. He came. He stayed. He gave his life for them. My God what a man." (What a priest!)

Prayer for Beatification of Fr. Mazzuchelli

"Lord Jesus, you called your servant, Samuel, even in early youth, to leave home and all for a Dominican life of charity in preaching your holy gospel. You gave him abundant graces of Eucharistic love, devotion to your holy Mother of Sorrows, and a consuming zeal for souls. Grant, we beseech you, that his fervent love and labors for you may become more widely known, to a fruitful increase of your Mystical Body, to his exaltation, and to our own constant growth in devoted love of you Who with the Father and the Holy Spirit live and reign one God, world without end, Amen."

2: God's Bridge of Love to Others

In 1982, the *Dubuque Telegraph Herald* newspaper conducted a survey to name the new bridge that connected Dubuque, Iowa, With Wisconsin and the Diocese of Madison.

The name "Mazzuchelli Bridge" received the most votes, perhaps because of ways Venerable Father Samuel Mazzuchelli influenced early Illinois, Iowa, and Wisconsin. It was then submitted to the Dubuque City Council, but the council named the new bridge the Dubuque-Wisconsin Bridge instead.

God's Bridge of Christ-Like Love

The bridge was not named after Father Mazzuchelli, but in my judgement, he was already God's bridge of Christ-like love to Catholics and non-Catholics in Iowa, Wisconsin, Illinois, and upper Michigan.

As God's bridge to others, father Mazzuchelli reflects many of Pope Francis' qualities. Like him, he was a bridge of God's mercy, love, and justice to the oppressed.

He defended Catholic soldiers' rights to attend Sunday Mass at Fort Mackinac, Mich. He wrote to government officials protesting injustices against Indians and settlers. He opposed slavery and condemned the Civil War's bloodshed.

Like Pope Frances, Father Mazzuchelli was a bridge of Christ's mercy to the sick and dying. In 1850, a cholera epidemic struck New Diggings, Wis. He buried the dead and he transacted wills and bequests hastily made by doing Protestant and Catholic parents. He took responsibility for orphans. He has a special place in his heart for orphans, probably because his mother died when he was six and some of his early classmates were orphans.

Bridge of Peace Between Faiths

Father Mazzuchelli was a bridge of peace between Catholics and others. He lived when religious controversy was an accepted fact of life. Though he didn't agree with some of their beliefs, he respected and was respected by Protestants, Masons, and others.

In 1862, when Benton's Primitive Methodist Church was destroyed by fire, Father Mazzuchelli sent $25 to help rebuild the church as proof of his goodwill. The $25 dollars was greater than the St. Patrick's collection for six months.

Civic Leader and Builder

Like Pope Francis, Father Mazzuchelli liked people. To settlers he was civic leader, friend, and builder of the City of Man and City of God. Though Catholics were a minority, he was asked to serve as chaplain at the first Wisconsin territorial legislature.

He helped to design the Galena Courthouse, the Galena Market House, and the Lee County Courthouse of Fort Madison, Iowa. He also helped to build numerous churches and schools.

He Liked People of All Walks of Life

Father Mazzuchelli liked people. In Rudyard Kipling's words, he could "walk with kings, nor lose the common touch."

His friend, Judge Charles Corkery, wrote that "today Father Samuel could be found in the mansion of the affluent and tomorrow in the hovel of the poor. There he is, high upon the scaffold, with coat off the sleeves tucked up, industriously at work in brick and mortar. In the evening, you see him in the pulpit, discoursing on some abstruse topic, and tomorrow he lectures before governors, judges, and legislators.

"In some ways, he reminds me of Fr. Mathias Wernerus, who built the Dickeyville Grotto near my home."

Recognized Women's Gifts

Father Mazzuchelli also recognized women's gifts. His vision of American Dominican life was realized by the Sinsinawa Dominican Sisters, whom he helped found.

On August 18, 1848, when the Sisters were novices, the Wisconsin legislature granted them legal status to incorporate the Benton Female Academy. The Sisters retained full legal authority and ownership of their property. Bishop James Shannon wrote that it's hard to name a group that has done more to Christianize and civilize the Midwest than these thousands of religious women.

Christ-Like Master Teacher

Like St. Dominic and many religious Sisters, Father Mazzuchelli was a Christ-like master teacher. He wanted the Sisters to actively teach and not be a cloistered community. When he learned that they were asked to do more domestic work than teaching, he protested. The Sisters were permitted to spend more time in teaching. It is fitting that the Dubuque Catholic Mazzuchelli Middle School was named after him.

At the Benton Female Academy, Father Mazzuchelli was respected and loved by the Sisters and students. Students remembered how he enjoyed seeing them have fun, share sleigh rides, and giggle with girlish joy. In the hearts of Sisters and students, Father Samuel (as he was called) was a superior person, always kind, simple, humble, and approachable.

Marking 150th Anniversary of Death

On February 23, 2014, we will celebrate the 150th anniversary of his death. During the year, there will be pilgrimages, special Masses, and other activities too numerous to share here.

Addendum

1: Stress

Stress seems to be a modern problem. Spring, the season of renewal, offers us opportunities to unwind, relax, and renew ourselves in ways that reduce stress.

Stress is not new. In Mark 6:31 it says that people were coming and going in such great numbers that it was impossible for Jesus and his disciples to eat.

We see stress's effect by holding a glass of water. It won't be heavy if we hold it a short time; but, if we hold it for an hour, our tired arm drops to rest. The same is true of stress. We need to put it down so we can rest. When we are rested, we can pick it up again and it will be lighter.

Competition, jealously and mistrust can cause stress. Today married couples often try to balance their challenging role of mom and dad with many other responsibilities that can cause stress. Stress can lead to child and spouse abuse and even divorce.

Stress robs us of sleep, suppresses our immune system and makes us vulnerable to illness. It can decrease our efficiency at work and cause us to act in un-Christian ways.

We need to accept responsibility for creating or maintaining stress and if necessary, change bad habits. We can relieve stress by accepting what we can't change and making time for fun and relaxation. Laughing at ourselves reduces stress.

Sharing lunch, a stimulating conversation or enjoying friends who listen and affirm reduces stress. Soothing music, watching an inspiring movie or enjoying a nap helps to relieve tension. To reduce stress, we can look at the bright side of life and focus on what is going well. We can keep a journal. We can go for a daily walk, ride a bike or join a gym.

When we are stressed, we may reach for unhealthy high calorie, high fat, and high sugar foods. Improving diet with healthy foods such as fruits, vegetables and protein helps reduce stress. We can leave work at work. With today's technology, it is so easy to stay connected.

We can relieve stress by disconnecting for a while. It's amazing how much this relieves stress.

Fear of failure, disappointing people, not meeting another's expectations or envy of another's gifts often leads to stress. Instead, appreciating our God given gifts and using them to love God, our self and others reduces stress. Realizing daily that we are loved by God and others reduces stress and helps us to love our self, God and others.

Prayer can help to relieve stress and live better. In Matthew 11:28 Christ says, ""Come to me all you who are weary, and I will refresh you." Let us accept Christ's invitation and enjoy God's gift of today. What we do with today can be our best gift to God today and tomorrow.

2: Humility

Don Shula was an outstanding coach for the Miami Dolphins. After winning the world-famous Super Bowl, he went on a vacation to Maine with his family. It rained which spoiled the fishing. So, the family decided to see a movie in the local theatre. When they walked in, the six or seven people in the theatre stood up and gave them a standing ovation.

Don Shula responded, "Thank you. I didn't think anyone up here were Miami fans. I really appreciate this."

The apparent leader of the group replied, "Mr., we don't know you from Adam. The reason we cheered was because the theatre manager said that she wouldn't show the movie until at least ten persons showed up. You and your family made it twelve. Now, we can see the movie!" It was a lesson in humility for Don Shula and his family.

In Matthew 1:29 Jesus says "Learn from me. For I am meek and humble of heart!" What does it mean to be meek and humble of heart? Does it mean to put ourselves down? Does it mean to think too little of ourselves? Does it mean deny our true worth?

Humility is not thinking little of ourselves at all. In its most profound sense humility means being like Jesus, who said, "Learn from me for I am meek and humble of heart." Humility means to be like Jesus, who said the Son of Man did not come to be served, but to serve and give his life as a ransom for many.

Humility means to live as Jesus lived, not for ourselves but for others. It means to use our gifts and talents as Jesus did, not for selves, but for others and their needs. The humble person acknowledges that they have gifts, but these gifts come from God and to God be the glory. He or she thanks God by using their gifts to help make the world a better place.

A famous Bible scholar said that that the best translation of the Bible was his mother's translation. She helped to translate the bible into everyday life. Jesus challenges us to translate God's Word into everyday life. He challenges us to use our talents not for ourselves and our own glory but for others and their needs. "I shall pass through this day, but once. Therefore, if there is any good that I can do, God, let me do it now. Please show me how. For I shall never pass this way again." Help me be humble, now, please!

3: Resentment

Years ago, as I worked on this article on resentment, my computer asked, "Do you wish to delete resentment? Press delete!" I chuckled and said that I wished it were that easy! Deleting resentment in our lives takes time and the grace of the Holy Spirit.

In Matthew 18:22, Jesus tells Peter that we are to forgive someone who wronged us, not just seven times, but seventy times seven times.

Christ placed a high priority on forgiveness because we are created in God's image. Since God is love, we image God best when we love; but our ability to love has been wounded by sin. Therefore, we need to forgive and be forgiven so we are free to be more loving persons. In the Our Father, a courageous prayer, we ask God to forgive us as we forgive others.

Resentment can hurt our ability to forgive and love! It often begins when someone hurts us by a slanderous remark, a friendship betrayed, being bullied or betrayed or other sins. Our natural instinct is to retaliate either in thought or deeds.

When we recall the hurt that someone caused, the hurt feeling may rise up again, enslave us, magnify the original hurt and make it difficult to forgive! A hurt that is brooded over has a life of its own that feeds off our anger. Dr. Martin Luther King said that resentment multiplies hate. According to Fr. Eugene Hemrick, resentment is the major psychological and spiritual addiction of all time.

Jesus said, "Love your enemies and pray for those who persecute you." William Barclay, the Protestant clergyman and Bible scholar stated, "No one can pray for another and still hate that person."

Christ showed us how to love, redeemed us from sin which hurts our ability to love and sent the Holy spirit to empower us to love as he loved. He forgave his executioners from the cross. In Colossians 3:13 it says, "Forgive whatever grievances you have against one another. Forgive as Jesus has forgiven you."

A woman got into a big argument with her brother over something trivial, but which escalated into a civil war. For years she and her brother resented each other and were unable to forgive each other. Their dying mother begged them to forgive and be reconciled. When they did, they were inseparable. Her brother died in her arms. She gratefully said that these were the best years of her life and forgiveness made this possible.

We can deal with resentment in many ways. First, we can face our resentment squarely, discover its causes and try to respond in a positive way to control and limit it. Second, we can forgive ourselves. A close friend, spiritual director, or counselor can sometimes help us to face up to our resentment. There is an old saying that when we share with a compassionate friend that joys are doubled, and sorrows cut in half. Third, we need to realize that resentment often hurts us more than the other person and wounds our ability to love. Finally, coping with resentment can motivate us to come closer to God. On its deepest level, forgiving others is an act of love toward those who have been unjust or even betrayed us.

Let us ask God to help us do what we cannot do ourselves, namely, to forgive someone who hurt us so we are free to image God by the ways we love each other, especially the least of God's people.

4: Hospitality

A couple with four small children who were new to the area arrived late for Sunday Mass. All the seats were taken. Consequently, the couple had to stand alone in the back of Church. No one offered the mother and her baby a seat. Apparently like Mary and Joseph, there was no room for them in the inn of their hearts. The woman's arms became numb from holding their baby. Her husband dutifully guarded their three other children who were little whirling dervishes.

Unexpectedly the baby began to cry. People stared at them as if they had committed a mortal sin. The mother was so angry that she decided to walk out. Before she could, an usher and his wife rescued them.

"My wife and I are sorry that we didn't see you sooner," the usher apologized. "We will bring cushioned chairs for you and your children." His wife added, "We'd like to treat you for coffee or juice and donuts after worship." The couple and their children gladly accepted.

The usher and his wife's hospitality motivated the couple to join the parish. Their kindness was magnified because it was given to strangers in need. The usher and his wife believed that Jesus showed them hospitality by inviting them into his kingdom. They passed on his hospitality by welcoming the couple as Christ welcomed them.

In Hebrews 13: 1-3 it says, "Brothers and sisters: Let mutual love continue. Do not neglect hospitality, for through it some have unknowingly entertained angels." Hospitality was important in the Old Testament because in the desert, one could die if they did not receive hospitality. Jesus gave hospitality to friends and strangers and welcomed them into the kingdom. Jesus will continue to offer hospitality through us if we let him. The stranger that we welcome may be one of us.

Pastors and preachers share hospitality by their preaching, presiding, tone of voice and by verbally welcoming parishioners, newcomers and visitors. The hospitable congregation makes sure that the church is comfortable, clean and has sacred space that invites graced worship.

Hospitable church members share hospitality when they pray for each other, offer rides to church and visit parishioners and others in nursing homes. They share hospitality by attending funerals, sending condolences, simply moving over in their pew or giving up their seat to a stranger in need. They are hospitable, courteous and Christ-like to others in the parking lot. They reach out to suffering persons, give to collections for the needy and more.

In an article entitled "Hospitality at Church" students were asked to attend different churches. The twenty-year-old's reported that the churches they liked best were hospitable. A church has hospitality when collectively it never forgets that 24,000 people die every day from malnutrition, and it tries to help when it can. A church has deep hospitality when it remembers that the Biblical command to "love your neighbor" appears in only one place in the Hebrew Bible while the command to love the stranger appears in more than 30 places. The New Testament word for hospitality is philoxenia which means "the love of strangers."

A parish that has hospitality remembers how Mother Teresa, when invited to receive the Nobel prize in 1979 honored the Biblical tradition by insisting that the ceremonial banquet be cancelled and asking that the 6000 dollars cost for the banquet be donated to the poor in Calcutta. The money saved on that banquet would help her feed hundreds for one year.

The church of hospitality is not only welcoming to visitors and strangers on its doorsteps but is ever mindful of Jesus' instruction to consider the poor, the crippled, the blind, the lame, and the stranger beyond that doorstep, those who cannot repay.

When I help at parishes, I appreciate hospitality from ushers, sacristans and ministers of hospitality. However, hospitality is not limited to them. All church members are called to be hospitable. It is an act of love that breaks down walls and opens doors to friendship. It takes effort, sacrifice and may inconvenience the giver. But hospitality shouts to those who receive it: "You are welcome here. We are privileged to have you at our home, our table or church." Parishioners should offer hospitality to each other because sometimes today many parishioners are strangers to each other.

Christ-like hospitality is a foretaste of the welcome that we hope to receive at the end of our earthly life in heaven. In Matthew 25:34-35, Jesus says, "Inherit the kingdom prepared for you from the foundation of the world. For I was hungry, and you gave me food, I was thirsty, and you gave me drink, a stranger and you welcomed me."

Acknowledgments

I thank those who, often without knowing it, encouraged me to persevere in writing. These include the Beloit Catholic High Arista newspaper, Diocese of Madison Catholic Herald, other newspapers, TEC newsletter, Veronica Deane, Sister Mary Paynter, Bishop William Bullock, John Berg, Knights of Columbus, Sister Lolita, Delia Schoeder, and especially Tim McKearn and Mary Jo Loeffelholz. Thanks to Jean McKearn for collecting and arranging the articles into a seasonal format; and to Forty Press for publishing this book.

About the Author

Fr. Don Lange was born in Louisburg, Wisconsin, a town of less than 100 persons. From that small town came four priests in 25 years. He was ordained to the priesthood on May 23, 1970. God willing, he hopes to celebrate his 50th Anniversary to the priesthood on May 23, 2020.

Fr. Lange graduated from Wisconsin State College – Platteville with a major in English and secondary education and a minor in History. At graduation, he was awarded the Elmer McNett Award for English. He went on to graduate from Holy Apostle's Seminary in Cromwell, Connecticut; St. Francis Seminary in Milwaukee, Wisconsin; and St. Mary's College in Winona, Minnesota. He graduated twice from St. Norbert's Theological Institute and attended four-plus more years of religious workshops.

Fr. Lange played baseball and softball for about fifteen years and coached baseball on all levels for 42 years. He has completed a marathon, and despite arthritis, participated in numerous senior softball throws. Before arthritis hit, he enjoyed biking and walking.

Fr. Lange has always enjoyed being a priest despite its occasional challenges. He especially enjoys preaching, presiding at Mass, writing, and telling and writing children stories.

www.ingramcontent.com/pod-product-compliance
Lightning Source LLC
Chambersburg PA
CBHW020928090426
42736CB00010B/1078